PRAISE FOR
BREATHE TO SUCCEED

"Science has validated the power of breathing and mindfulness to enhance our well-being. Sandy Abrams's advice is a simple but incredibly effective way to make mindfulness a part of your life and help you thrive in our always-on world."

—Arianna Huffington, founder and CEO
of Thrive Global

"Mindfulness is transforming the business world due to the positive impact it can bring to both individuals and organizations. *Breathe to Succeed* contributes a range of strategies for individuals to begin to integrate mindfulness into their routines and to use as a tool in everyday life."

—Emily Winer, mind concept lead at the
International WELL Building Institute

"In today's 24/7 digital world, where we face more stress and distraction than ever before, Sandy Abrams's breathing techniques are immediately actionable ways to remain focused and calm. They help me to perform at work especially in intense situations, which has a positive effect on the colleagues around me."

—Nick Goode, executive vice president for
produc

D1056828

"Employee burnout is a real thing; we've all heard the stories, read the scientific research to support it, and watched the impact to the bottom line. Sandy's book provides easy steps on how to incorporate mindfulness and breathing techniques into lives to restore balance within ourselves. As a proud employee of an organization that supports well-being in the workplace, I am honored to recommend this book."

—Dawn Runge, PhD, SPHR, and SHRM-SCP, HR executive value advisor at SAP SuccessFactors

"Our breath . . . it's free and always with us, no matter the situation. Backed by research and compelling real-life stories, *Breathe to Succeed* teaches us how to harness our breath as a powerful resource for well-being, productivity, and performance."

—Jannell MacAulay, PhD, Lt Col, USAF retired, leadership and performance specialist, and mindfulness advocate

Marissa,

BREATHE

TO

SUCCEED

Let's Breathe!
Inhale, Excel...
Much success!
♡ Sandy

BREATHE

Increase Workplace Productivity,

TO

Creativity, and Clarity through

SUCCEED

the Power of Mindfulness

SANDY ABRAMS

CAREER
PRESS

CONTENTS

INTRODUCTION

Fear is excitement without breath.
—ROBERT HELLER

How you think and feel is a choice—a very important choice that should not be left to chance. You have the power to choose and therefore own some control over your destiny. To a large measure, your thoughts and energy can help create the life of your dreams because positive thoughts and energy foster positive outcomes whereas negative thoughts and energy tend to forecast negative outcomes. It's science. You'll see "It's Science!" pop-ups throughout the book that share the science-based research behind the power of breath and mindset. Without conscious breathing, your thoughts can default to negativity and doubt and become self-sabotaging. Instead, connect your mind and body to the kind of thoughts and energy that will bring the success you desire. Breath is a ready and available vehicle for transformation at any given moment.

Even just three deep breaths can be truly transformative: from fear to excitement, from nervous to calm, from doubt to certainty. When you breathe mindfully (even briefly), you get the benefits of meditation without having to sit still for long periods of time. You can breathe to succeed in small snippets every day. Make the decision to choose your thoughts and energy as often as possible and you'll quickly begin to see the incredible power that you have within.

When was the last time you took a long, slow, deep breath? Most people can't recall. Treat yourself to one deep breath right now. Ready? Take a really long, deep inhale and a long, slow exhale. Ahhhhhh. Let it set the tone for you to relax into this book with an open mind about the power of breath for success. Taking control of your thoughts and emotions through breath will add tremendous value to the way you lead and/or work. Whether you're an executive, an entrepreneur, an employee, a leader, a CEO, a colleague, or a team player, tapping into the power of your breath will open the door to a new level of clarity, creativity, positivity, productivity, and abundance, and a new sense of calm strength and connectedness.

Three deep breaths (3DB) and a variety of other simple breath techniques can easily be your superpower for quickly taking control and shifting your energy, mood, and perspective whenever and wherever you need empowerment. In the moment. No more shallow breathing all the time. It's not serving your body or your mind, and it's certainly not elevating your energy for success and business. Get ready to upgrade your breath and take control of your thoughts, emotions, and energy. No more autopilot. Breathe to succeed.

It's Science!

In an article titled *Neuroscientists Have Identified How Exactly a Deep Breath Changes Your Mind,* Morgan Cerf of Kellogg School of Management Northwestern University says, "Breathing at different paces or paying careful attention to the breaths . . . were shown to engage different parts of the brain. Humans' ability to control and regulate their brain is unique: e.g., controlling emotions. . . . These abilities are not trivial. When breathing changed with the exercises, the brain changed as well. . . . The findings provide neural support for advice individuals have been given for millennia: during times of stress, or when heightened concentration is needed, focusing on one's breathing or doing breathing exercises can indeed change the brain."[1]

This book is my love letter to breath. It's about sharing the transformative power of breath in business; how even 3DB (three deep breaths) at key moments can be nothing short of miraculous. I'm not your typical meditation teacher. I'm an entrepreneur with a business sensibility about meditation . . . and *breath is meditation at the speed of business!* I hope to empower you to utilize easily accessible and very effective breath techniques as meditation in the moment, in under sixty seconds. That's doable, right? If your thoughts and emotions have been controlling you, that can change right now.

Mindful breath completely transformed my life in 1989 when I began practicing yoga. I became obsessed with breath and the way it could immediately shift my thoughts and energy. After six years of daily practice, I decided to complete a yoga teacher training program (not to become a teacher but to deepen my knowledge) and have since done well over 10,000 hours of yoga and breath practice. *Breath is meant to go beyond the yoga mat.* Breath has saved me (from myself!) in business for over twenty-five years. It always delivers. It never disappoints. It'll do the same for you. Breath will be the missing piece of the puzzle in fully (or finally) connecting your mind and body. No yoga required. Again, how you think and feel is a *choice*. When you breathe mindfully, you move into your optimal performance zone with limitless potential because you're in sync with your mind, body, and beliefs. In the chaotic business world we live and breathe in today, we're constantly multitasking under extreme pressure, deadline, and distraction.

When we're in work mode without pause, it's dangerous both emotionally and physically and leads to burnout, stress, damaged relationships, and the habit of never being present.

> *Fear and doubt limit everything; breath expands everything, including opportunities, performance, positivity, and success.*

Taking mindful, deep breaths paired with positive intention (I call this *Breathing Like a Boss*) is the fastest and most effective way to literally connect with your mind and body and *choose* to feel the way that you want to feel—in a way that will lead to accomplishments, goals, and your version of success. Breath is not esoteric or abstract . . . *it's science!* As you begin to experiment with your breath, watch as your default perspective becomes positive, patient, and clear to make mindful decisions and to be productive, creative, open-minded, and present unlike ever before. We often aren't conscious about how we let our negative thoughts and habits lead the way until it's too late; we've made hasty decisions and/ or acted impulsively with colleagues, employees, supply partners, or customers. Breath will become your new compass, the emotional GPS that is always activated to guide you in the best direction. If you're practicing it regularly, the benefits will likely seep into your personal life too. How's that for value?

IT'S SCIENCE!

Josh Axe, a certified doctor of natural medicine, a doctor of chiropractic, and a clinical nutritionist, says, "Life today doesn't often offer us the opportunity to enact a full stress response and resolution. Instead, we operate as if we're in a constant, low-grade state of emergency, with no real end in sight. Many of us don't physically dispel stress hormones or take the time to resolve the real problem . . . or to question our priorities."[2]

My perspective on utilizing breath for success comes from my twenty-five-plus years as a small-business entrepreneur. However, the advice here is not only for entrepreneurs; it's relevant and empowering to employees, intrapreneurs, corporate leaders and executives, people who work at home, teams, freelancers, consultants, and so forth. In fact, as Jason Feifer, editor in chief of *Entrepreneur* magazine, recently explained, we are all entrepreneurs. The term has evolved; he writes that "[t]he old definition was attached to a small business person but today, the word entrepreneur is different. It means a mindset, a culture, identity. It means someone who makes things happen for themselves. You can do that in any form; you can be an entrepreneur and not own a company, you can do that in your life or at a company you work for. It's a mindset for people who seize opportunities and create things . . . ."[3] Mindful and strategic breath will definitely help seize opportunities and create ideas, products, energy, and success. Whatever your title may be, we are all the CEO of our own mind–body connection. When we activate that connection with breath, we become what I call a "C.E.'Om."

There are a few common reasons why people are quick to say, "I don't meditate." Often, the initial effort can feel futile. I can relate to many reasons that I've heard, and that's why my breath techniques offer game-changing benefits without the high barrier to entry for what we think of as meditation. Simple breath practices invite you to experience meditation in ways that are immediate and offer instant results rather than frustration. Here's why *Breathing Like a Boss* will begin to work for you right now:

1. It takes less than sixty seconds at a time to tap into the power of quiet and stillness. You'll see as soon as you take 3DB.

2. Breath can help short attention–spanned, fast-paced people (like me) learn how to slow down internally.

3. I have a business sensibility about breath, so my advice is practical, functional, and efficient, not New Age-y. (Burning incense gives me a headache and I feel awkward chanting Sanskrit phrases.)

4. It's a practice that doesn't require getting to a certain level of enlightenment or prerequisite training. It's understandable that many people try meditation once, get frustrated, and say, "It doesn't work." They get analysis paralysis wondering if they're doing it correctly, so they move on. *Breathing Like a Boss* is a personalized practice that's accessible in smaller snippets throughout the day as it meets you exactly where/when you need it most.

Three deep breaths (3DB) have been a superpower to help manage my daily thoughts, emotions, and energy in order to reach my goals *and* enjoy the process; learn from my failures/mistakes; and continue to evolve. It's often your mind (rather than your ability) that limits your success. Enhanced breath cuts through that limiting and negative thinking and ushers in positive strength to go beyond where a negative mind would have you throw in the towel. Mindful breath is easy to activate and insightful to experience whether you're in a challenging moment or you simply want to be present. It can be seamlessly integrated into whatever your day looks like. Managing our thoughts and emotions is something that we may never completely master. I mean, we're human. But we don't want to be haphazard with emotions in business. We can train ourselves to live in our highest energy more often than not. Knowing that you have the power to reset at any time is like being handed the keys to the kingdom (of our mind-body connection). Once activated, you can *Breathe Like a Boss* throughout your workday with a new sense of freedom, confidence, and control.

My secondary intention with this book is to be part of the larger conversation unfolding right now about the effects of technology on our health and wellness. Our constantly connected business lives are causing health concerns that need to be addressed with a sense of urgency. Of course, being immersed in tech is an absolute necessity of business, but we need to add in a larger humanity quotient and set new boundaries. Breath, self-awareness, and small changes in our daily routine can be a big part of the wellness solution. We are ten-plus years past the dawn of smartphones (and social media), and those of us who have been connected since then are getting or have already gotten to the tipping point of being digitally overwhelmed. This situation is only going to worsen if we don't build awareness to ensure our digital well-being.

We've recently learned that the engineers of our favorite social platforms designed them for users to become addicted. Mission accomplished, right? I feel like we might be in the "saccharin of sweeteners" phase of technology, not knowing how dangerous our behavior is because the science isn't quite there yet. We can't wait for the science to fully catch up. It's time to get proactive. Take charge. While breath has been saving me in business situations for over twenty-five years, it has also more recently been an incredible antidote for my frequent feelings of brain fog, digital overload, and distraction.

This simple and impactful practice of *Breathing Like a Boss* will elevate your business life. My goal is to introduce the concept, prove my case, and then have you become your own teacher by making the practice uniquely yours. Empowering yourself. It's fully accessible, starting right now. Enhanced breathing and positive intentions will help you soar to your next level of success and connect you where you most need to be connected now—to your mind and body. Let's breathe on purpose, with purpose . . .

1

THE (UNDERUTILIZED) POWER OF BREATH FOR SUCCESS

When you own your breath,
nobody can steal your peace.
—ANONYMOUS

Before I had my "aha" moment for a beauty product idea and built it into a multimillion-dollar business (Moisture Jamzz), before I wrote my first small-business guidebook (*Your Idea, Inc.*, Adams Media, 2009), and before I built my entrepreneurial/small-business consulting business, the only thing I was known for, way back in 1989, was "the girl who always left yoga class right *before* Savasana." Sanskrit (an ancient language of India) for "corpse pose," Savasana is the last pose of yoga class where you lie still for several minutes. Being still made me anxious. Savasana seemed like a complete waste of time. I'd stare at the ceiling as my mind swirled into to-do lists and my heart set off to race. I saw no value in those last five minutes of class. I had places to go and people to see. I had no respect for stillness. I wasn't wired for it. "Namaste, see you tomorrow!" I'd nod to the teacher and slip out the door sideways.

Slithering out of yoga class pre-Savasana was a total rookie move that was offensive both to my teachers and the practice of yoga. It was also a disservice to my mind and body. But at that time, I wasn't capable of questioning my disdain for stillness or even to simply recognize the value of those precious moments at the end of class. The teachers began to pull me aside and ask why I bothered making the daily effort (sometimes twice a day) to attend yoga class but left before it was over. They'd kindly urge me to complete the traditional practice. Instead of faking it, I decided to try to experience what they all considered the "most important pose." When it was time for Savasana, I awkwardly stayed on my mat with eyes wide open, but I wasn't finding any answers in the ceiling fans, so I closed my eyes. Only there, in my internal darkness, was my body finally moved to take a long, deep breath, allowing me to quietly settle in. How was it that one simple deep breath could magically ease me into a "space" of centering that I had never arrived at before? Ever.

That powerful yet peaceful place where I could be still and quiet and absorb all the goodness of the practice . . . *that* was Savasana. Aha! Savasana is the reason that we do an entire yoga flow class in the first place— to get to a place where our mind and body can happily be still. Instead of Savasana making me tired, as I feared it would, it was completely rejuvenating. It felt like my mind and body were holding hands and smiling. I felt whole and connected, focused and energized. *Therein was my truth;* when I owned my deep breath, I could connect my mind and body and take control of my pace, my mood, and my attitude . . . on *and* off the mat. The indelible lesson of simple deep breathing had been formed and I'd never look back. Breath is an extremely underutilized tool for success. We have to do it to stay alive, and yet, the tool remains untapped in the lungs of stressed-out, overworked people all over the globe. I hope to change that, one deep breath at a time. I'm compelled to share my story of breath and its full effect on my entrepreneurial life in hopes that doing so will help many others in business on so many levels. Not everyone has the capacity or desire to do long-form meditation, but we can all tap into the empowering benefits of 3DB (three deep breaths) as meditation.

IT'S SCIENCE!

Crystal Goh, an affiliate at the Applied Neuroscience Lab, says: "Findings show a system where our in-breath is like a remote control for our brains: by breathing in through our nose we are directly affecting the electrical signals in the 'smell' regions, which indirectly controls the electrical signals of our memory and emotional brain centers. In this way, we can control and optimize brain function using our in-breath, to have faster, more accurate emotional discrimination and recognition, as well as gain better memory."[4]

Three deep breaths (3DB) has given me more inner strength than I could ever have imagined. 3DB is the best way to begin to get to know the power of your breath. Once you begin to *own* your breath, you'll never have to experience a challenge on your own again. Your breath will always be with you to support and empower. I initially shared my enthusiasm for breath in 1998 when I wrote my first article in the spa industry magazine *Pulse*. In my article, titled "02 Breathe!," I shared my experience with breath after almost ten years of practice and told how it sustained me in business and in life as a new mom. But in that pre–social media time, there was no engagement after it published and I was busy building a business, so there was no further conversation. Now that meditation is mainstream and the business sector has become what it is today, the timing could not be better to share my (even deeper) enthusiasm with breath for success.

When you enhance your breath, you connect to your mind and body, and this connection allows you to be in sync with your positive and strategic thoughts to "breathe your goals to life." With mindful breathing, you'll begin to access everything inside you that will have you performing at your highest level, feeling a sense of control and limitless potential. It will bring more value than you can fathom at this moment. Improving your breath and mindset is what leads you to finding and exemplifying attributes of success. Qualities like patience, persistence, confidence, nonjudgmental behavior, clarity, creativity, and compassion are easily accessible through breath and will help tremendously in business. When you're moving from a place of inner strength and positive intentions, you solve problems easier, make better decisions, have clearer lines of communication, and build a culture of respect that leads to long-term success.

EMPOWER YOURSELF WITH BREATH

Breath can be your closest comrade in the battle of business. It will always be with you as a first level of defense against what can be the most brutal force on the field: your own (negative) mindset. Breath facilitates that connection to finally liberate you from feeling driven by habitual negative thoughts and emotions. There's a vulnerability that entrepreneurs face while trying to juggle all aspects of a business until we have the means to either fully learn a process or bring in people who are strong where we are weak. Until then, we have to learn to roll with the punches as new and unusual situations arise daily. We can find empowerment from *Breathing Like a Boss* to get back up each time we feel defeated.

Stop the drain.

Breathe in the power.

Get back up with renewed energy and determination.

Breath summons your inner strength to find a better way.

Breath directs you to let go of the defeat and not be defined by it.

Breath brings you back to the enthusiasm of your original purpose/passion.

Breath allows you to take (back) control.

When others tell you that your ideas sound silly and ridiculous, when the manufacturer that you need is nowhere to be found, when your comments aren't being heard in a meeting, when you've been overlooked for a promotion, when someone else got the sale or took the opportunity, when you get that sideways look that makes you feel completely inept or ignorant when you're just trying to learn something—breath is the tourniquet.

Enhancing your breath from the automatic shallow breathing pattern allows you to control your energy by connecting to the corresponding part of your brain that regulates emotion. (More in Chapter 2 about the power of the mind.) Tal Ben-Shahar, PhD, says, "Shallow breathing is a reaction to the unyielding stress of modern life—and is itself a cause of further stress, which leads to more shallow breathing."[5] You may lose many fights, but you're in it to win the battle, right? You can begin to fill the well of doubt or negativity with each deep breath. Shallow breathing brings shallow results.

BREATH IS THE NEW MEDITATION

Sure, it seems that most people want to meditate; they like the *idea* of it, but there's a real disconnect between wanting and doing because of the time and effort involved to just sit still. Meditating for a full session every day is a difficult sell for many, let alone the stereotypical Type A's with short attention spans or an overworked and time-crunched employee, corporate leader, or entrepreneur. Breath is the first step. Meditation is frequently thought of singularly in regard to finding enlightenment and feeling Buddha like—calm and chill—but it's so much more. One deep breath can be considered a meditation. It's science; it's not mystical. *Breathing Like a Boss* covers a big swath that includes not only calm and chill but also a plethora of other positive emotions to help you take charge, accomplish your goals, and up the ante with productivity.

It's Science!

In an article titled "How to Detoxify Your Body," Tal Ben-Shahar says, "Your lungs are important detoxification organs that are often forgotten. When you breathe, they absorb oxygen from the air and expel carbon dioxide from your body to keep your red blood cells functioning. The better your lungs can take in oxygen and remove carbon dioxide, the more energetic you'll feel and the better your body will function . . . ."[6]

Enhancing your breath is ground zero, the perfect place to begin to feel the benefits of meditation without having to reserve a chunk of time or master the art of stillness. It meets you where you are. *Mindful breath is meditation at the speed of today's on-demand business life-style.* There's abundant power in even one deep breath, but 3DB is still my go-to several times a day. It's my reset button and nobody's even the wiser. You can be completely inconspicuous while you're regrouping your energy. 3DB is an easy way to begin to experience the power of your breath and the freedom and strength that it brings. Imagine how much better and more productive your work will be when you begin to take advantage of mindful breath. With each deep breath you inhale, you can bring in something positive while letting go of what's holding you back with every exhale.

As with meditation, many different types of breath techniques are available as well as endless ways to enhance them. (Learn more coming up in Chapters 2 and 3.) You can begin and end with 3DB (three deep breaths) and still have life-changing results. Or you can dive deep and go wide. I look at breath practice in the same way that I see entrepreneurship: we all need to find our own unique way by *doing.* I hope to open your mind to the idea that owning your breath can be completely transformative and easily integrated into your day to add a sense of ease in reaching your goals and enjoying your journey to full-blown success—whatever that means to you. We all have different ideas of what success is, so be true to yourself. Finding clarity on *your* meaning of success will also become easier with breath practice.

IT'S TIME FOR YOU TO BREATHE LIKE A BOSS!

If you let a negative mood or energy ruin your day, that's usually when things go awry, right? It's when we experience the broad, intense range of emotions that business can evoke (sometimes all before 10 A.M.!) that it's up to each of us to stop, refuel, and refocus with breath. We forget (or may not have ever fully understood or believed) that how we think and feel is a *choice*! Without my breath practice to help tap into my confidence and inner strength back when I was launching my business, I definitely would have given up at several difficult milestone points. But I chose to breathe, stay positive and strong. I had to.

Without breath and mindfulness, I wouldn't have been able to ignore the salesman at the fabric cutting company who chuckled and condescendingly told me that my order was way too small for their production requirements. I stopped in my tracks because I needed reinforcement. I could easily have said something nasty and stormed back to my car, but instead, I took my 3DB, refueled with positive intention (and some chutzpah), and calmly marched with purpose around to the back cutting area to speak with the manager. I confidently pleaded my case for smaller minimums; I needed help meeting current demand but had to start small. Apparently, the manager saw potential and made an exception. That felt much better than the alternative. I went on to become one of their biggest customers. Breath.

Simultaneously, without the power of breath and positive mindset I wouldn't have had the fortitude to walk in and out of well over fifty sewing contractor offices while struggling with a language barrier to find the right match for my difficult-to-sew product. Mission accomplished, but it was long after I would have given up if it weren't for my breath as a guiding force. I still have one of the original sewing contractors from those (difficult) days working with me twenty-five years later. Breath. Without my breath practice priming me before important phone calls, I never would have sounded confident enough to talk with big corporate buyers. I landed a large chain store account before I even knew what "PO" meant. Seriously. I was outside of the business world; my degree was in broadcasting journalism. "Purchase Order" wasn't in my lingo yet. When the buyer mentioned it, I had to quickly call my friend who was in sales for the translation. You don't know what you don't know, so *sounding* confident can go a long way until your confidence actually comes from experience. Breath also helped me through many challenges with technology at times of complete frustration—from learning electronic data interchange, or EDI (electronic methods for purchase orders and shipments), to later dealing with things like algorithms and search engine optimization (SEO). Innovations in technology make it pretty difficult for non-techies like myself to keep up with digital marketing. Tech in the digital marketing space was unlike most other aspects of bootstrapping where a small business entrepreneur can fake-it-till-you-make-it. Breath.

Energy that is positive, clear, and confident allows for the kind of mindset that will make better decisions, and it's our daily decisions (even the ones that *seem* small) that lead us closer (or further away) from our goals. Breath brings tenacity for endurance and long-term persistence. It never gets old, and it's always empowering. So many things are out of your control every day at work, so utilize the one thing that you *can* control—your breath and therefore your thoughts, emotions, energy, and actions.

BREATH IS READY WHEN YOU ARE

Breath will meet you right where you are. No need to hold onto the stress, anger, or frustration and wait for the evening gym workout, run, or yoga class. You'll still get there, but you can begin to manage your situation right away with breath. Nobody knows exactly what you need to hear in a challenging moment better than *you* do. Begin to silently speak up to yourself in the moment. Show up for yourself. Tell yourself that you're going to be fine, that you *can* do it, breathe slowly and deeply with the intention of mustering up your inner strength.

It's in there; breath will bring it to you. Exercise classes are awesome—I'm a big fan of the collective energy of a daily yoga class—but for the other twenty-three hours of the day, *you* are your best teacher and biggest supporter. Take the inspiration from classes and personalize it. That's where the "aha" moments happen; the real transformation happens inside. *You* are in control of your thoughts and emotions. 3DB and you can "turn on a dime." No need to wait for an outside source to recalibrate and turn a bad situation into a win.

When you learn how to be self-aware (coming up in this chapter) and upgrade your breath, you'll make mindful business decisions rather than hasty ones. You'll build meaningful long-term business relationships rather than simply conduct transactions. You'll tap into your creativity instead of just working from random or mediocre ideas. You can expand your energy and mindset by activating different kinds of breathing techniques and swapping your automated shallow breath for higher-performance oxygen while detoxifying your body at the same time. Breath is the catalyst that will begin to change the way you reach your goals. You'll communicate with your brain and instruct it to help your mind and body think and feel in a way that will lead to expansion—more success, more opportunity, more abundance. You *can* take control. It's hard to imagine how something so simple can be so transformative.

BREATH IS FOR SUCCESS . . . AND WELLNESS

There's an SOS that I'm hearing loud and clear within the business sector. We are a little over a decade into using smartphones and our fully immersed digital business lifestyle has no real boundaries. We are expected to be available 24/7/365 . . . and we don't always mind! Maybe it's an excuse to have our eyeballs attached to our screens. Maybe we enjoy the distraction. Maybe we're addicted. Maybe we love what we do. Regardless, this connected lifestyle can lead to a warped sense of busyness that's easily mistaken as productivity *and* constant connectivity leads to low-level chronic stress.

> *Our minds are constantly distracted. Our attention spans are severely shortened. We want everything on demand. Our inboxes are never empty. Our energy is frequently negative. We're addicted to social media. We're sleep deprived and anxious. Sound familiar? This cannot and should not be the new normal. Breath to the rescue for wellness too.*

Technology is only going to continue to increase in our lives, but we have human needs and limitations that need to be managed. Experts have said that our brain and body are not designed for this current lifestyle of excessive screen time (more on this in Chapter 4). The power of breath can answer this SOS and bring much-needed relief to refocus and manage our digital stimulation and distraction. It's in moments of enhanced breath that you can feel like you're in Savasana basking in the goodness of silence and stillness, recovering and recharging. Utilizing your new favorite breath technique at key moments in business will make you more mindful and productive. Breath is at your beck and call. Breath also has compounded benefits that stick around long after each exhale.

It's Science!

Dr. Andrew D. Huberman, professor of neurobiology and ophthalmology at Stanford University, says, "Breathwork can be thought of as exercise in that, if done correctly, has immediate benefits—physical, emotional and cognitive but breathwork also has longer-term benefits if you do it regularly. . . . The idea is that people can alter and strengthen the neural pathways that link breathing with emotion regulation centers in the brain, which can help them feel calmer, more alert, and sleep better, depending on the protocols they use."[7]

SELF-AWARENESS COMES FIRST

Self-awareness begins by understanding who you really are and discovering (and accepting) your personality traits, mental habits and patterns, and where and when you tend to be weak or negative so that you'll know exactly when and where to add positive reinforcement through breath. Self-awareness means becoming an observer of your own thoughts, behavior, and energy. Our mindset and mood can easily steer us in the wrong direction at any given moment, but we can nip it in the bud with breath. As you begin the self-awareness process, be open to seeing yourself in a *nonjudgmental* way. It's best to realize the truth so that you can make changes and improvements. Also, be aware that where you may feel weak today can be improved with self-awareness. Don't think of your weaknesses as personality defects; they are simply traits that you haven't yet reformed.

You might be surprised at how long you've let old, toxic, and limiting beliefs take up residence in your mind. It's time to evict. The stop-gap can come in the form of even just 3DB and a simple positive thought or intention. Building self-awareness is like having your own mindful security team who will be there to stop negativity when it gets too close. You may not typically spend even one minute thinking about your mental state, energy, attitude, or anxiety level when you are reacting to all of the tasks that need to be taken care of in one typical day at the office. That needs to change. I like the way Tony Robbins defines this self-awareness that we need to hone in on: "Self-awareness is one of the rarest of human commodities. I don't mean self-consciousness where you're limiting and evaluating yourself. I mean being aware of your own patterns."[8] This awareness becomes very important as you begin to utilize breath for success.

Don't worry; after a while it becomes second nature and "self-awareness check-ins" serve as the positive reinforcement that you *are* in control and aware of the way you think and feel. You'll begin by consciously tuning out outside stimuli and turning inward briefly and consciously so that you notice both how you feel and what you're thinking at various times during the day. You'll begin to clearly identify your negative tendencies. In his Harvard Business Review article titled "How Leaders Become Self Aware," Anthony K. Tjan says, "There is one quality that trumps all, evident in virtually every great entrepreneur, manager, and leader. That quality is self-awareness. The best thing leaders can do to improve their effectiveness is to become more aware of what motivates them and their decision-making. Without self-awareness, you cannot understand your strengths and weakness, your 'super powers' versus your 'kryptonite.'"[9]

You already know the physical feelings of stress that your ongoing negative emotions can elicit: the knots in your stomach; the proximity of your shoulders to your ears; the clenching of your jaw; the nagging neck pain; or the on-edge, tightly wound feeling that you could snap if someone looks at you the wrong way. Noticing your *thought* patterns is also part of the process. Maybe you can even begin to see that when you're having negative dialogue, you feel accompanying physical annoyances. Notice the correlation. Many people have a constant negative loop happening in their heads that may sound something like, "I can't do this. There are much smarter people doing similar things. I don't have a degree in this. I don't have enough money to do this. It's such a long shot. I should save myself the pain. . . ." (These certainly sound familiar!) Letting negative dialogue drive your decisions is a dangerous daily practice that will inevitably lead you in the wrong direction, and on top of that, your stress continues to simmer. When you're steeped in your negative thoughts, you begin to have a tunnel vision for only the negative situation and limit your potential of seeing other positive possibilities and opportunities.

For example, if you wake up feeling overwhelmed by a complicated project, you can *choose* to focus only on how difficult it's going to be, or you can *choose* to be positive and focus on a variety of solutions that you're enthusiastic about considering. This shift is where the transformation of energy happens, and it happens through breath. You can begin to stop the madness by becoming self-aware of your destructive patterns and replacing them with positive habits. It's a choice.

GETTING TO KNOW YOURSELF AND OTHERS

Self-awareness is necessary for building high-quality relationships (with teams, employees, colleagues, vendors, manufacturers, and customers), which really are the biggest asset of a business. Getting to know yourself also helps make you more curious about getting to know others. How well do you know the people you work with and/or do business with every day? Knowing more about someone's backstory allows for real connection and a better understanding of what's important to that person. People like sharing their stories. Take a few minutes here and there to get to know people better. When I spent a lot of time exhibiting at trade shows, I realized that every entrepreneur has a unique, interesting, and often surprising and poignant backstory. Whenever there was downtime at a show, I'd walk around and ask people how and why they began their business. I found it super inspiring, and it made me want to support a company once I understood the passion and sweat equity that went into it. I also spent many years recently writing about entrepreneurial stories on the HuffPost website. When you read inspiring stories and see a piece of yourself in someone else's journey, it can spark confidence and momentum. You can also learn from other people's mistakes.

MANAGING NEGATIVITY

When I first began to build my business, I'd post inspiring quotes above my desk on a (pre-Pinterest) bulletin board. One of my favorite quotes was from self-help author Peter McWilliams: "You can't afford the luxury of a negative thought." It kept me in check with the mind–body connection that's critical for success. It came in handy more times than I like to admit since it *is* a luxury to allow yourself to feel negative because that's easy. You can resign yourself to the rejection or the fact that you probably aren't going to be able to do something because it's *hard* or it requires more than you think you may have inside you. Wallowing in negativity is a normal default, but it affects your mind, energy, and confidence, therefore affecting the outcome of your efforts in that same negative way. Often we don't realize how much negative conversation we allow ourselves to silently conduct every day in our mind. A big percentage of our daily thoughts are both repetitive and negative, and they are sabotaging our efforts. Hence, we *cannot* afford the ease or comfort of residing in that place of defeat or negativity. Just as we need to know the numbers in our company's profit and loss statement, we also need to know what our mind and emotions look like to see exactly where and when change needs to be made. Although these are two very different things, both are critical to success. Breathe.

Activating your self-awareness comes right before activating your breath. Self-awareness will help you sense and understand when you feel in need of an energetic shift or boost. You'll stop for a second and *realize* that you're thinking negatively, feeling anxious and fearful, or moving from a place of chaos, impatience, or frustration. Once you become aware, you make the change with breath. When you learn to sense negative energy in your body and then have the self-awareness to know that you need to change it, that's when breath becomes an important part of your daily routine. In fact, it can change your routine habits into powerful rituals for success.

The process of self-awareness grows faster each time you use it and becomes embedded in your mind as a new habit. You're empowered to sense, notice, and then swap counterproductive thoughts and feelings for a higher level of energy through your intentional deep breaths. When you take deep breaths, you oxygenate the blood, which causes your brain to release endorphins to trigger a positive feeling that also helps to reduce stress. Bingo. It's all working together!

IT'S A PRACTICE

I'd bet that if asked, most people who know me well would describe me as happy and calm. I certainly don't always feel that way. Sure, I love "happy and calm," so I work at feeling and *being* that way. I know the feeling in my mind and body when I'm in it, and there's nothing better. But if left to my own devices, I might default to other standard settings that I've brought in during my adult years. I'm a worrier. I'm fast-paced (that's a nice way of saying I tend to be impatient). My mind is always moving. I have a short attention span. I'm a future-based thinker. But I know that the magic happens when I'm self-aware and present in the moment. I confront my chaotic energy head on and slow it down with some deep breaths to keep me "happy and calm." Mindful breathing and positive mindset are ongoing active practices that really have changed me . . . and my nervous system.

Breathing Like a Boss has moved me closer to the energy that I had when I was younger and more of a free spirit, but life happens and we become responsible adults. We all know that best version of ourselves that often gets pushed away in order to focus on work. The goal is to live in our positive energy more often and be our best selves even when things get crazy. When I work on being present, confident, and certain, that's when I get my best ideas, my creativity is in complete flow, and

I hear the word "yes" in abundance. With each practice session of breath, you're breathing *into* something new, with a new thought or perspective. Or you're breathing *through* something that will continue to change. With each exhale, you're breathing something *out*, letting something go. Some element is always a little different than the day before. Your mind and body are always changing, so 3DB will always feel fresh and empowering. The practice is about learning, growing, and evolving with your breath and your mind–body connection. You are developing your keen sense of self-awareness and getting to know and appreciate your inner self with each deep breath.

MAKING THE PRACTICE YOUR OWN

One of the absolute best things about breath practice is that it's *yours*. You don't need anyone's permission, acknowledgment, or guidance. You'll evolve with your practice in the way that works best for your mind, body, and personality—knowing that however and whenever you want to activate your breath, that's the right way for you if it's making you feel more productive, more present, and clearer. You'll learn to develop your own habits and rituals for both self-awareness and breath practice that will empower you over and over again. Breath is a guiding force that feels like putting on new glasses and finally being able to clearly see both close up and into the distant future. As you become familiar with the power of breath and the power of your mind (see Chapter 2), you'll experiment and get uniquely creative with your breath practice. Personalizing your breath makes you want to tap into it more and more. There's no right or wrong way to utilize your mind–body connection to do better, feel better, and think better. Use breath in a way that wakes you up inside and empowers you to be the best version of yourself. *Own your breath so that you can own your peace!*

SELF-AWARENESS SAVED ME FROM MYSELF!

Not long after launching my business in 1993, my patience was tested big time. I had a large chain-store buyer interested in placing a purchase order larger than I imagined. I was so excited to get this order in motion (before she changed her mind!) that I became very impatient to seal the deal. I wanted to offer a discount to incentivize the buyer to have a sense of urgency. I knew that I needed to wait it out, especially because she hadn't complained about the price, but I knew that price was a big part of the negotiations. From being self-aware, I definitely knew that I had a tendency to be impatient and that it *never* served me well. Every morning I turned to my breath for patience; it became my ritual as

I waited. It stopped me from calling the buyer and nudging or offering that random discount. It helped shift my focus onto something else. I knew that if I acted on my impulses, not only would it look totally amateur but it could also jeopardize the whole deal. I had to breathe into my patience and have faith in the timing. Knowing where I fell short, I was able to bring in reinforcement through breath to focus on the bigger picture goal of building a mutually beneficial long-term business relationship while being mindful in the process and keeping my stress level in check. I was able to hold tight until the buyer responded with that dream purchase order. Breath worked and the launch of this new partnership felt so rewarding. This big chain turned into a twelve-year relationship. If I had been impulsive and offered even a small discount in order to expedite the deal, it would have cost me hundreds of thousands of dollars over the years. I'm grateful for being self-aware and calling on my breath to save me again and again.

LEARNING TO LISTEN TO OURSELVES . . . AND OTHERS

As I became more self-aware, l realized that listening to my own internal voices made it easier to listen better in general, too. Like many, I wasn't always fully present in a meeting or a conversation, but where I really noticed that I fell short was while exhibiting our products at trade shows. The pace is frenetic, and it's common to juggle having to talk with a few different people at once. I had a tendency to semi-listen while toggling back and forth between conversations, trying not to miss a question or have anyone leave the booth without fully understanding our products. I was leaving business on the table by not being fully present to connect one on one with potential buyers. It left me feeling frazzled as well. I decided to change my trade show habits, slow my pace while in the booth, and focus when someone was speaking to me. One at a time. First come, first served. My breath kept me in the present moment and made me a much better listener, which led to developing meaningful, long-term business relationships, understanding the customer's wants and needs and closing deals on the spot. Buyers felt understood. And guess what? People *waited* to talk with me because they could see that I gave individualized attention. I cared. Listening is an important part of success in business, and it doesn't come easy with a fast-moving mind that lacks self-awareness.

In addition to trade shows, meetings are another place to consider listening skills and notice the habits of others. Can you imagine how much more productive meetings would be if everyone was listening intently? Learning how to be present and fully listen opens so many more doors, too. Observing meeting etiquette is an interesting exercise. Are people listening for the end of someone's point to immediately jump in and add something of their own that has nothing to do with acknowledging the last comment? Not truly hearing all the feedback during a brainstorming session or conversation limits the full potential of a group's collective energy. Coming to the table ready and willing to listen changes the game. Maybe meetings should begin with 3DB, a basket for phones to be put in, and an intention to focus on what's being said so that no idea goes unexplored. All in favor of this, say aye!

STEP ONE WITH SELF-AWARENESS

An easy way to gain some self-awareness is to take a personality test online. One of the most popular tests is the Myers-Briggs (*www.myersbriggs.org*). You can take a similar one for free at *www.16Personalities.com*. I enjoyed doing this exercise and in case you're wondering, I'm considered an ENFJ type. If nothing else, these tests give you insight into a variety of character traits that you may not even realize have held you back in business. Doing these tests or even just writing a list of your strengths and weaknesses can help you grasp aspects of your personality that you need to watch and be able to intercept. Learning to be more self-aware of your detrimental habits will speed up the process of reversing their effects. A study by the American Management Association revealed that "A high self-awareness score was the strongest predictor of overall success."[10]

Here are some situations that you can change with self-awareness. If you see them happening, you can now stop, take 3DB, and talk yourself out of your usual behavior so that you can overcome the tendency to repeat self-sabotaging behavior:

- Are you a perfectionist who works on things ad nauseam and never finishes because they're not good enough yet?

- Do you multitask and then not remember what you just did?

- Do you procrastinate on difficult tasks?

- Do you need results immediately rather than see the value of process?

- Do you take feedback or constructive criticism personally and negatively?

- When one thing goes wrong, do you then feel out of control and expect that everything else will go wrong the entire day?

- Do you ignore your gut instinct because you don't feel confident?

- Do you tend to be a creature of habit, sticking with a bad situation way too long because you fear unknown change?

Consciously changing your breath is about managing your energy. Enhanced breath expands your energy. When you shift from negative to positive energy, it's noticeable on the inside because it brings a sense of health and wellness to your nervous system. The change can also be felt and seen by others. You know how good it feels to be around people who are positive and supportive, compassionate, and kind? You can be one of those good-vibe people, too. I've been an eternal optimist and pretty intuitive my entire life, although I have questioned my intuition at various times and have since built a specific breath practice to fix that when I feel out of touch with my gut instinct (learn more in Chapter 3). I'm grateful to have some sort of mechanism that connects me to choose to change when I feel out of sorts. Self-awareness is not a switch that you can immediately turn on; it's a process and an eye-opening experience. You may have absolutely no idea that you've been one of those people who tend to be naysayers and need to focus on transitioning from a default of negative to positive. And by positive I don't necessarily mean happy; we can't be happy all the time. By positive, I mean that you feel strong, centered, focused, and optimistic and have clarity for the time being—even if that clarity means that you feel frustrated or upset. You don't have to let that emotion go unresolved. The self-awareness is about noticing the problem and then figuring it out from a better perspective after you've breathed through it a bit. You'll likely be amazed at how you begin to crave these self-awareness check-ins.

WHAT DOES A SELF-AWARENESS CHECK-IN LOOK AND FEEL LIKE?

Checking in with yourself is not a long internal dialogue or a lengthy process; it's more like a high-speed scan of your mind and body. It's similar to noticing if there's a tiny pebble in your shoe, or noticing that your button-down shirt feels awkward because the buttons were done on the wrong holes. The minute you sense something negative in your scan, it immediately becomes something you can't ignore any longer and you have to reset. It's your own bio-feedback hack. It's simple:

- Stop and be still.

- Close your eyes.

- Take three deep breaths.

- Scan your body for typical signs of stress: clenched jaw, tense hands, headache, stomach in knots, feeling your heart race, shoulders up to your ears, etc.

- Listen to your thoughts. Anything negative being said in there?

- Take a few more deep breaths to settle in for the initial check-in.

Make a mental note to yourself and begin developing a sort of allergic reaction to your own familiar signs of stress. They will no longer be tolerated. Negative thoughts will be replaced with deep breaths and positive intentions. The next time you feel those signs of stress or hear those uninspired voices, you're going to immediately stop them. You're going to breathe them right back out. You *know* when you're in need of uplifting energy; it's just that you usually ignore the signs and keep moving from a place of habit. Self-awareness is a pact with yourself in which you commit to not living in that negative space anymore and understanding that your best ideas, decisions, and actions occur when you are in a healthy state of mind–body connection through breath.

A FEW IDEAS TO BEGIN YOUR SELF-AWARENESS CHECK-IN HABIT

Any one of the following suggestions may be enough for you to begin integrating this new habit. If you want to add extra reinforcement, go ahead and use more of these:

- Program reminders on your phone for two-to-four times per day to stop and check in with your mind–body. Definitely include upon waking and one before going to sleep. Starting and ending your day *Breathing Like a Boss* helps keeps the cycle going strong.

- Attach the check-in to another activity that you do regularly like eating, drinking water, and walking to the restroom, or when you would otherwise scroll your Instagram feed!

- Scan your mind–body when you get your caffeine fixes. Deep breaths can often replace that late afternoon caffeine that can mess with your sleep.

- When you get into your car, instead of imme-diately turning on the radio or podcast or mak-ing a call, enjoy some silence and check in with yourself. Take 3DB and bask in the quiet space. Let go of anything you don't need and clear your mind. Your car (or train ride or walk) can serve as another opportunity to go inward.

> ## IT's SCIENCE!
>
> In a Harvard Business Review article titled "What Self-Awareness Really Is (And How to Cultivate It)," organizational psychologist Tasha Eurich says, "Self-awareness seems to have become the latest management buzzword—and for good reason. Research suggests that when we see ourselves clearly, we are more confident and more creative. We make sounder decisions, build stronger relationships and communicate more effectively. . . . We are better workers, who get more promotions and we're more effective leaders with more satisfied employees and more profitable companies."[11]

With so many benefits to self-awareness, it's something most people need to work on because Eurich also says that only a small percentage of us (10%–15%) fit the criterion of being self-aware. Let's get on that bandwagon. There's also a wonderful bonus to self-awareness where you begin to see the *source* of negative emotions and stress. You might begin to take the initiative to eliminate the source of the repetitive stress rather than having to breathe through it over and over. We begin to see incredible changes from taking action on what we learn through these quick check-ins.

IT'S TIME TO TAP INTO YOUR BREATH!

There's only so much you can learn from reading, and as with launching a business, you need to start by *doing*. So let's cut to the chase again for 3DB right now. Let's continue to to unlock the power of your breath. Don't overthink it. Just take a long, deep inhale starting from your belly. Close your eyes or leave them open if that makes you more comfortable. I recommend inhaling through your nose. Exhaling through either your nose or mouth is fine. Breathe in all of that untapped, uplifting energy. Then exhale just as intentionally and slowly. Savor the change in your body and mind. Appreciate the nourishing feeling. Second breath: Whatever it looks like, take it. It's about the *doing*, the starting to change, creating a new habit, activating your dormant breath and practicing. Three's a charm, right? Inhale deeply. Exhale it all out. Ahhhhhhhhh! You're beginning to own your breath . . . and your peace. Everything's better with breath. Every single thing. If you're going through a challenging business situation, breathe *through* it in the moment right when your body begins to produce those stress hormones. On the flip side, if you're enjoying an incredibly successful moment, breathe *into* it. It'll help you enjoy being present and embed yourself in the moment to produce the feel-good neurotransmitters. It's that versatile. It can push you through something and lend energetic support, and it can make you more present to fully enjoy a victory. It can also do so much more—you'll see. Begin to take more deep breaths everywhere—while you're driving, waiting, typing, reading, listening, in a meeting, walking. You get it. There's never a bad time for deep/mindful breath, and whatever you're doing is only going to become better, more thoughtful, more focused, more YOU.

You've unlocked the power of your breath. It's like uncorking a wine bottle; you can never go back, and why would you? Let breath become your secret weapon in business. Let it lead the way. Let it power you through obstacles, challenges, and decisions. Let breath clear your mind and reset your internal chemistry so that you can be the best version of yourself in business and beyond.

2

UNDERSTANDING THE POWER OF YOUR MIND

It all begins and ends in your mind. What you give
power to has power over you, if you allow it.
—LEON BROWN

Now that you see how breath will help manage your energy and improve the way you interact in business, next up is understanding how your breath connects with your mind to unlock and expand your true potential. What you *think* about is a critical part of success. Heightening the level of self-awareness about your thoughts and understanding the power of consciously connecting to your mind (through breath) will help you reach your goals fast and easy. When I think of examples of a strong mental game, Tiger Woods comes to mind. He was known for his mental toughness as a golfer from a very young age, thanks to his father's military background introducing Tiger to a discipline that other young golfers simply didn't have. It gave him a clear advantage. Individuals being able to perform under pressure in sports never cease to amaze me—like seeing those last-second buzzer-beating baskets made from mid-court. How did they do that? They *know* they can. That inner strength and awareness of your mind–body connection will be a tremendous asset in business too. If you didn't begin focusing on your mental game during childhood like Tiger, don't worry—it's never too late to rewire your brain and form new disciplines and empowering habits. You can begin now with breath. You're not stuck with any negative pattern; you can always replace it.

IT'S SCIENCE!

Dr. David Bach, a Harvard-trained neurologist and founder of the Platypus Institute, says, "If you interrupt a neural pathway consistently, over and over for thirty or forty days, that pathway will actually dissolve—even if it's been in the brain for decades."[12]

When you make the mind–body connection, you'll see how it can feel to be effortlessly in sync. Manifesting positive thoughts, intentions, beliefs, and emotions and then attaching those to your breath is a multiplier for the effectiveness of your breathing techniques (breath techniques coming up in Chapter 3).

Breath offers incredible benefits on its own, but when the mind is involved and your breath is powered by well-intentioned strategic thoughts, it can be exponentially more rewarding in bringing your goals to life.
The sky's the limit! This is the beginning of moving from thoughts to action with confidence, inner strength, and clarity. Get ready to breathe your way into next-level success.

We'll begin by scratching the surface (in simple terms) behind the power of your mind and how to utilize breath to connect. The breath–brain connection is a partnership that shouldn't be ignored. Breath facilitates curating the kind of thoughts that will produce meaningful changes. Let's begin to nourish your brain with empowering thoughts.

THE BREATH "MULTIPLIERS"

When I decided to start my business, I bought some business books but found them more intimidating than helpful because they were written by MBAs or professors. I didn't understand the lingo, so I turned to self-help books like those by Tony Robbins and Deepak Chopra and began to understand and believe in the power of positive thinking. The missing link for many people is how to tap into positive thinking if it doesn't come easily. Breath is the bridge. Once I paired my breath with empowering thoughts and intentions, things got very interesting. This section describes four tools that make your breath even more effective for ushering in productive thoughts that fuel your brain and optimize creativity, clarity, and determination. I call them multipliers: *"Acting As If," closing your eyes, visualization,* and *mantras.*

1. ACTING AS IF

"Acting As If" is a powerful "mind game" or technique that I learned in my early twenties at a workshop for success in business. The concept came at a perfect time for me to understand that my body doesn't know whether or not my mind is telling the truth, so if my mind says, "I am successful," I can begin to mentally and physically believe that I am successful. Your body will feel that good energy when your mind tells it to. The "Acting As If" technique brings in the aspirational feeling of having already gotten to that place of reaching your goals. On the flipside, the negative stories that you may have told yourself over and over become part of yourself, too, but breath will help you change those stories once you realize that *you* control your thoughts. If you keep thinking and acting as if you are *not* ready for a new opportunity or *not* qualified to follow a dream, then your body will act accordingly. And who wants to "act as if" from a place of lack and insecurity? Breathe out the old and breathe in the new momentum-fueled energy.

> *Mind is the Master Power that molds and makes, and we are mind. And ever more we take the tool of thought, and shaping what we will, bring forth a thousand joys, or a thousand ills. We think in secret, and it comes to pass, environment, is but our looking glass.*
> — JAMES ALLEN

It's poignant to think about that quote, right? You can use it for momentum in moving forward and focusing on thinking and acting in ways that create an environment that you're excited to work/live in.

IT'S SCIENCE!

Susan Reynolds, author of *Fire Up Your Writing Brain*, says, "Your thoughts form your character, how you operate in the world, how far you travel mentally, physically, and spiritually. You are what you think you are, and all of your actions proceed from thought. Your inner thoughts will always be reflected in your outer circumstances, because self-generated changes in your life are always preceded by changes in the way you think about something. As far as your brain, every thought releases brain chemicals."[13]

2. CLOSING YOUR EYES

IT'S SCIENCE!

"Inspiration may be more likely to strike when we close our eyes or simply stare into space. Creative ideas seem often to appear when we close our eyes, stare at a blank wall, or gaze out of a window—all signs of shutting out distractions and turning attention inward." From a study on NIH.org titled "Sudden Insight Is Associated With Shutting Out Visual Inputs."[14]

Our creativity flourishes when our mind isn't focused on something in particular. It's the easy, open mindset that produces the best atmosphere for creative ideas to come to life. The *idea* of closing your eyes seems so simple, but the act of closing your eyes is powerful and completely underrated. Most people open their eyes upon waking up and then only close them again when going back to sleep. That should not be the case; taking the opportunity to close your eyes with a few deep breaths throughout the day offers deep, on-the-spot rest and rejuvenation. I never realized the power of deep breath *and* closed eyes until I was in my Savasana breakthrough. It's something you need to consciously experience during a deep breath (or three) so it doesn't get trivialized. In addition to helping with creativity, closing your eyes will make you feel as if you're shutting a virtual door to everything outside of your body. You can quickly connect to your mind and body. When you limit the distractions that you see in your physical surroundings, you make it easier for your brain to rest. You can feel the change immediately. I consider that inward space my center, and it always brings a sense of being grounded and calm. Deep breaths with eyes open is still good, but check for yourself and see the incredible difference. Try it now if you'd like. Close your eyes and take 3DB. That inner dark space will become a welcome respite from the speed of business.

3. VISUALIZATION

> *Everything is created twice, first in the*
> *mind and then in reality.*
> — STEPHEN COVEY

Visualization adds yet another layer to the power of your breath. Visualization is a detailed and experiential way of thinking positive, taking your thoughts to the next level by seeing them like a film in the theater of your mind. Many people have a tendency to think about the obstacles when envisioning a goal, but doing so will limit you. Make the switch to picturing the successful end result instead. When I attended the "Act As If" workshop in 1992, I was a newbie real estate agent, lacking confidence and experience. I learned to go beyond just thinking about a goal to visualizing detailed scenarios of what I was hoping to do. For example, I'd visualize myself driving to a coveted listing appointment, dressed for success and in my dream car. Then I'd walk myself through the conversation, answering client questions confidently and closing the deal. I was showing myself the high-def version of me that I knew was waiting to emerge in time, with experience. Until then, I could breathe and believe. Utilizing breath along with visualization helps to embed the feeling of the desired scenario. I did different visualizations daily and worked hard to gain the experience and confidence of my future self who lived in my head. (Those scenarios eventually came to life!)

Take a moment to think about one of your dream scenarios at the moment. Visually create it. Take some slow deep breaths as you think about it. Are you accepting an award for a distinguished accomplishment at work? Giving notice at your job to pursue your entrepreneurial dream? Speaking at an industry event? Reaching a milestone goal with your team after an arduous process? Walking into a big chain store and seeing your own product on the shelves? Whatever it may be, visualize it fully and *feel* those emotions of being in that future moment. Just as there's something powerful about putting pen to paper and writing down goals, there is power in seeing something in your mind's eye. Your brain believes your story and your body goes along for the ride.

Visualization can also be done to *clear* your mind when it feels like you have a few too many "tabs" open. You can begin by focusing on just one thing. You might try visualizing the stream of your breath entering and exiting your body as you take a few deep inhales and exhales. Or you can visualize one color as you close your eyes and go inward with a long, deep breath. See yourself literally erasing the chaos into a clean slate of sky blue or white clouds. Another idea for breathing into a clear mind is to focus on your "happy place"; transport yourself mentally to *that* place, creating a go-to thumbnail image that you know will move your mind into a calm and open space. After a few times it won't require any effort—you'll immediately be transported when you decide to clear your mind. Visualization is a powerful way to see and feel your thoughts.

4. MANTRAS

Mantras are another impactful tool for your mind when paired with breath. Mantra is a Sanskrit word that combines the word "man" (which means mind) and "tra" (which means a vehicle or instrument). A mantra is a word or phrase (of your choice) that can help transport the mind from activity to silence or from negativity to momentum. A mantra can be repeated silently to help with concentration and make you believe and feel what you're repeating to yourself. It can expand your mindset and shift your perspective immediately. In my breath practice, there are no rules for choosing a mantra except that it has to be positive. Sometimes I use just one word that I want to manifest while closing my eyes. I will attach the word or emotion that I'm trying to manifest to long, slow deep breaths. As you begin to say (and even visualize) the words, you can feel them embed in your mind and body. Here are some single-word possibilities to begin with: Abundance. Success. Ease. Courage. Confidence. Patience. Vitality. Strength. Truth. Leadership. Find that one word that describes what you desire today.

Using the phrase "I am . . ." in front of your chosen word is frequently done in meditation practices. I am confident. I am capable. I am successful. I am financially secure. I am a mindful leader. I am ready. Saying "I am" is taking ownership and gets you right into the now. It may even add a little skip to your step. A positive new mood or perspective is just one deep breath and a mantra away. Give it a try now if you feel like it. Pick a word above or one of your own, close your eyes, see the word, and take 3DB. "I am . . ." "I am . . ." "I am . . ." Feel it. Own it.

You can also string together your own sentence that can feel more like an overarching goal. Maybe something like this: "I am determined to take one step today that will get me closer to . . ." "I'm willing to go outside my comfort zone and take a leap of faith in business today." The combination of words is endless and completely customizable. Get as specific as you'd like; add names and situations. Again, there's no right or wrong way as long as you're positively intentioned. The words can also be changed up any time, or you can stick with one mantra for weeks or months until you've reached your goal.

"People who are optimistic react to setbacks from a presumption of personal power. They feel that setbacks are temporary, are isolated to particular circumstances, and can eventually be overcome by

effort and abilities. In contrast, people who are
pessimistic react to setbacks from a presumption
of personal helplessness. They feel that setbacks
are long lasting, generalized across their lives,
and are due to their own inadequacies, and
therefore cannot be overcome."

— CHADE-MENG TAN[15]

You can *feel* the emotions that come about from those exercises; acting as if, closing your eyes, visualizing scenarios, and repeating your mantras. All four tools are simple add-ons that multiply the power of your breath to connect with your mind. These tools kick it up a notch . . . or two or three. You can mix and match those tools as you see fit.

IT'S SCIENCE!

"Beliefs are like 'Internal Commands' to the brain as to how to represent what is happening when we congruently believe something to be true. In the absence of beliefs or inability to tap into them, people feel disempowered. We have the power to choose our beliefs. Our beliefs become our reality." From "The Biochemistry of Belief" study[16]

ONCE YOU'RE CLEAR ON YOUR GOALS, CONSIDER DEVELOPING AN INTENTION

Intention setting is an empowering exercise that helps keep you on track in reaching your goals. Your intention will always be top of mind as the touchpoint for all decisions. Feeling strongly connected to your intention will add a new level of mindfulness to your work. Although goals and intentions are similar, goals are done under the umbrella of your intention. Goals change all the time as we reach them or pivot with new ones. An intention is more of an overarching statement of purpose for the big picture. Having a clear intention for your journey, venture, work, project, or business offers a sense of clarity for each decision along the way. Yvon Chouinard, founder of Patagonia, is one of my favorite examples of impactful intention setting. (His story is featured in Chapter 6.) Your overall intention is mission driven so that every action will be in complete alignment. This helps to set boundaries for not compromising when you're not finding exactly what you need and likely feel exhausted. Knowing that you want to stick with your highest intentions will give you reason to keep on going. When I launched my business in 1993, there was still a thriving garment industry in Los Angeles, but "sweatshop scandals" were beginning to make headlines both domestically and abroad. I wanted to be sure that as we built up our manufacturing system that we were intent on never being in this type of situation with our manufacturers. As we negotiated with sewing contractors, it was not all about the bottom line. It was the whole package: paying fair wages, knowing that working conditions were good and that quality was more important than quantity. I was determined to find a manufacturing partner who was transparent about their entire work environment and prided themselves on quality. It's important to share your intentions with business partners, colleagues, teams, employees, and customers. As I shared mine with possible manufacturing partners, it became obvious who was in and who wasn't interested in aligning with me. I wasn't going to compromise. Once the decision was made, I was able to stay on top of the situation by seeing it for myself in weekly deliveries and pickups, where I made a point to talk with everyone. Also, I was speaking not only with the managers, but with our sewing team. This was important because sewing gloves is a meticulous job and we were paying by the pair, so there was a delicate balance of speed, accuracy, and care. I had to be mindful of my overall intention as we finessed final minimum required quantities and pricing.

I also had another intention pertaining to the quality of our products, from our designs and fabric to the sewing, quality control, packaging, and customer service. We wanted every aspect to be done well and be something we were proud of at every interval in the process through the customer's use of the product. We were at the high end of pricing for moisturizing gloves because our intention was to make the highest-quality products that were also the only brand to be fully "Made in USA." Holding tight to our intentions made it easier at trade shows when buyers would inevitably ask why our gloves cost more (ahem . . . than the cheap plain ones that were made overseas and never fit anyone well). Without those clear intentions, I would have gotten defensive (as noted earlier), but instead I began to answer that question time and again with "I'm glad you asked." I happily shared my intention about focusing on the quality that goes into every step of our entire production process. The buyers appreciated hearing this, and the message and intention could then be conveyed to their customers as well. Having an intention gives clarity for each step of the way in business, whether you're on your own or part of a team.

Intentions are powerful because they are your "why," the purpose behind your actions. They're a foundational part of your journey in business. Developing your intention(s) can also include thinking about what you want to gain from your hard work or the legacy you'd like to build. If you don't yet have an intention for your work, take moment to think about it. Close your eyes and breathe through a few deep breaths thinking about what satisfies you and motivates you in business. What feels rewarding? What principles are guiding you? Write them down and continue to tweak as you come back to the process for clarity. Beginning to work with mindfulness is a whole different experience than just checking things off your daily to-do list without integrating some personal meaning. In a 2014 Fast Company article titled "Why Feeling Meaning at Work Is More Important than Feeling Happy," writer Jessica Amortegui says, "Increasing a sense of meaningfulness at work is one of the most potent—and underutilized—ways to increase productivity, engagement, and performance."[17]

TAKING IT ONE STEP FURTHER: BUILDING COMPANY CULTURE

Company culture is built from intentions, and it becomes the mindset of the office, team, and brand. One of the first examples where I learned about what company culture meant was reading Zappos CEO Tony Hsieh's book *Delivering Happiness* in 2010. He talked about how Zappos wasn't about selling shoes (which was all it sold at the time), but instead Zappos was delivering happiness. That was visionary. Hsieh had a clear intention of making happiness his company's top priority, and the company culture was built around that core tenet. Hsieh's intention for happiness wasn't just for customers; it was part of the office atmosphere as well. If an employee didn't jive with their culture, Zappos would pay them $2,000 to quit rather than not fit with the culture that included "creating fun and little weirdness, along with being positive, open minded, adventurous and creative." Hsieh says, "We've formalized the definition of our culture into 10 core values. Basically what we're looking for are people whose personal values match our corporate values. They're just naturally living the brand. Wherever they are whether they're in the office or off the clock."[18] The Zappos culture and intention paid off handsomely, selling to Amazon for $1.2 billion in 2009.

Starbucks CEO Howard Schultz has also said something in the same vein: "We aren't in the coffee business. We're in the people business. We just happen to serve coffee."[19] He had a clear intention of building Starbucks stores around being that "third place" in our lives, where we go in between home and work to experience community connection. It certainly was that way for years and then it *became* the office for many! Intention helps business owners or brands have clarity on the way they run their business. It may not even be something that customers notice overtly initially, but unconsciously it might be exactly why they gravitate to the brand—and stay loyal. You can use your breath sessions for finding clarity on your intentions and for generating ideas about building a company culture or aligning with your company's existing culture.

CAUSE-BASED BUSINESSES AND B CORPS

Being self-aware and setting mindful, meaningful intentions around company culture has led to a surge of cause-based businesses. TOM's led the way in that space with the "Buy One, Give One" business model. There's also a new community of brands called *B corporations*, which are brands that are certified as such for making a legal pledge to be a changemaker business. According to BCorporation.net, "B corps are for-profit companies certified by the nonprofit B Lab to meet rigorous standards of social and environmental performance, accountability, and transparency. B corps are creating a new kind of company that serves society and shareholders. They are using business as a force for good to solve social and environmental problems." Patagonia is a well-known B corp. It's a privately held company whose founder believes it will be around for at least a hundred years and he is determined to have his business philosophies, company culture, and legacy continue. Founder Yvon Chouinard says that "Benefit Corporation legislation creates the legal framework to enable mission-driven companies like Patagonia to stay mission-driven through succession, capital raises, and even changes in ownership, by institutionalizing the values, culture, processes, and high standards put in place by founding entrepreneurs."[20]

I interviewed Kickstarter co-founder Yancey Strickler a couple of years ago for a HuffPost article, and he said that the Patagonia brand story inspired them to make the B corp commitment as well. Strickler explained: "Becoming a benefit corporation is a new option for companies. It's a legal change in ownership status that requires us to produce a positive good for society. We lay out a charter to explain how we'll do that. We're supposed to do a private report every 2 years, but we'll report on it publicly every year starting February 2017. It's a legal mandate for our future course of action. We are quite excited about this because it will preserve a certain ethos and set of principles for the organization for as long as we have the privilege to exist, regardless of who management is. It locks in the idealism that the company was founded upon and ensures that it's always core to how we operate. It's a big step."[21]

BCorporation.net notes that there are over 2,500 B corp businesses now in over 60 countries spanning 150 industries. Consumers care more now than ever before about dealing with businesses that support good causes; we're willing to pay more if it helps a company's mission to solve social and environmental issues. It's a small way for each of us to feel like we're giving back too.

INTENTIONS WITH WORK–LIFE BALANCE

There's an ongoing discussion (we could even say argument) about the possibility of finding work–life balance. This discussion is even more important today, as we are constantly connected to screens and many people have no boundaries for separating work and life. As you establish your intentions for your work or business, you may want to consider your work–life balance intention as well. When I launched my business, I had no idea about building culture. After a year, our company consisted of myself, my husband, my mom, and one employee. Looking back, we did have a "family first" culture. I knew from day one that I wasn't setting out to build an empire, and I did have intentions about a lifestyle balance. I was building what had become a pretty big business, but my husband and I were also about to have our first child and it was important to both of us that we be present for our kids. My husband took a leap of faith in 1995 and left his law practice to help run the business with me. We set up our business out of the house (before working remotely was cool) to build the lifestyle that we wanted as parents. Without formalizing it, our culture was built around our intention to maintain a thriving business while balancing parenthood and focusing less on growth and more on maintaining the business we had built in the three years prior to having kids. Intention is important for a solopreneur or small business owners, too; it's not just for big corporate brands.

Having that clarity made it easy for us to err on the side of volunteering and attending school functions without any guilt for leaving the office on a busy day. Most of our work could be done outside of "business hours," anyway. We always knew that we could never get missed time with the kids back, and it was the freedom of working for ourselves that we loved more than the idea of building an empire. Now, as our kids are in their twenties we know that it was a decision we'll never regret. We were both home full-time with them and managed our schedules, prioritizing the way we had intended. Thinking about your work–life balance is important for relationships, stress relief, productivity, and wellness. Ask yourself if you are satisfied with your work–life balance or your "connected/unplugged" balance. (More on this in Chapter 4.) Breathe into this idea of balance for a few breaths. If you're one of those people who doesn't like the word "balance," maybe think about this in terms of priorities. Are you content about how you *prioritize* your days, weeks, months, and years?

POSITIVE MINDSET HELPS EXPAND YOUR ABILITY TO TAKE RISK

Having a positive mindset enables you to take risks and be more confident about them. The older I get, the more I can relate to the fact that it is the things that we *don't* do that we most regret. Success in business always requires some sort of risk. Arming yourself with empowering thoughts through breath practice will help you to get innovative and do things that you wouldn't have had the guts to do before. You're not working hard to be average, right? Taking risks can become more doable starting right now because you have the tools to get to a new place of inner strength to make a decision. Then you'll either make the most of it, or worst case, you'll recover from it. If you don't try, you never know—and that's a risk too. Your breath practice will help you greenlight decisions that you'd otherwise let pass by and possibly later regret.

CREATING YOUR OWN OPPORTUNITIES

It's empowering when you have clarity on the goals you want to achieve. Write down your goals. Then you can begin to work backward and figure out how to get from where you are to a specific goal. The first step can be the most difficult to take, but it's also the most exciting—and the most important. As Tony Robbins says, "You haven't fully decided until you've taken action." Take a small first step; it's momentum and it makes it real. A positive and creative mindset will lead to thinking outside the box in order to make things happen. Success often requires creating your own opportunities. When the right situation doesn't seem to exist, try to create it. This can be done by productizing an idea and selling it; that can be in the form of either a product or a service. Don't be afraid to reach out to people and share your creative idea or solution. Propose your solution; *ask* for the business. Be bold. Breathe into confidence. When you see a void in the marketplace or a void in your workplace, create your own unique opportunity, add value, and fill the void that people may not have even noticed yet. Create your own opportunities. This is how businesses launch, how promotions occur, how ideas turn into initiatives, and how products get to the shelves. You have to follow your goals and put yourself out there. *Breathe Like a Boss, choose your thoughts and energy carefully, and make things happen.*

CHANGING YOUR PERSPECTIVE CAN CHANGE EVERYTHING!

Being open minded is vital to being able to shift your perspective and open the door to success that wasn't available with your old state of mind. Changing perspectives allows you to reflect on an idea in a completely new way, opening the floodgates for a world of new possibilities. Ideas can then be generated by your own thoughts or from listening to other people's perspectives, even (or especially) if they differ radically from yours. Being open-minded will come as you expand your breath practice and use the power of your positive thoughts. Attaching yourself to one mindset about something can be very limiting and can hold you back from seeing a host of different solutions and opportunities. It's when you open your mind to a new perspective that creativity, innovation, and collaboration can happen. On the "Tim Ferriss

Show" podcast, Astro Teller (CEO of X, formerly called Google X) calls audacious big thinking "moonshot thinking," and says, "Perspective shifts will unlock more than smartness will." Teller says it's important to have collaborators from completely different backgrounds working together on finding solutions to big problems: "Like having Peter Pans work with Ph.D.s or aerospace engineers working alongside fashion designers."[22]

I've seen the power of unlikely collaborations first-hand on a tour of MIT Media Lab, where the "the crazier, the better" type ideas are welcomed and are being developed into future technologies that we can't even imagine. It's the convergence of unlikely teammates bringing unique perspectives that create magical solutions that could never have developed without shared perspectives. Surround yourself with a diverse group of people. Appreciate differences. Use your breath and your mind to shift your perspective and go big!

WHERE DO YOU USUALLY LIVE? PAST, PRESENT, OR FUTURE?

If you are depressed, you are living in the past. If you are anxious, you are living in the future. If you at peace, you are living in the present.

— LAO TAU

This is a good time to talk about the balance of being present versus thinking about the future all the time. "Acting As If," visualization, intention, and goal setting all have us living in the future, which is good in moderation. I'm a strong believer in having big picture and long-term goals so that you can plan accordingly, but being present is how you gain the most clarity and find the inner strength to continue on your journey to success. Make a conscious effort to live more in the moment, especially if your past experience isn't adding to your level of confidence and/or the uncertainty of the future makes you anxious. Often, fixating on your past is about holding onto something that was said or done to you that made you feel inadequate. If you have a certain situation "on repeat" in your mind's eye, begin to breathe through that story until it disappears. Refocus on your present mission and the fact that you're on a new journey. Be in a moment of gratitude, knowing that you've come a long way and that you're ready to set your mind to something bigger and better. When you're present, you feel grounded, strong, and connected. The fastest way to get present to take a deep breath. Even just one.

Celebrating little milestones along your journey is a terrific way to stay in the present moment, too. Otherwise, you're always focusing on the next thing and not acknowledging current achievements as they occur. I was guilty of this for many years, and it's not nearly as fun to be in a constant state of future-based thinking. Being in the moment will bring you more clarity for making better decisions, too.

MOVING INTO ACTION

Your strong and decisive mindset that will come to life through breath makes it easy to begin to take small, strategic steps every day that get you closer to your goals. The power of your mind and breath together is like soil and sun for plants. When you activate even small actionable steps, it's like planting seeds in your "garden of goals," which reminds me of a Robert Louis Stevenson quote that I had on my desk for years: "Don't judge each day by the harvest you reap but by the seeds that you plant." Plants take time to sprout, but if you plant the seeds, it'll happen. I still have to remind myself of this quote often because when progress seems slow, you have to be proud of the seeds you've planted and know they're slowly materializing. Your daily breath practice, paired with positive thoughts, helps build your confidence, upping your inner strength and fortitude—but it does, of course, require action! People can get too comfortable reading, planning, making lists, and consuming content; results come from executing on that knowledge in a reasonable amount of time. Once you're on solid ground with your foundation of a strong mind–body connection and your goals are determined, it's time to execute. You'll begin to see that your actions are much more strategic and focused because you're trying to get to the place that you *know* you'll arrive at because you've actually seen it, felt it (remember your visualization?), and completed your due diligence.

SIMPLE IS GOOD!

One benefit that I've seen many people experience with a newfound sense of clarity and a confident mindset is appreciating simplicity. There's a new feeling of gratitude for the simple things: the less complicated processes, the more direct communication, the back-to-basics approach for finding solutions. You may begin to notice how things appeared more complicated from a negative perspective—wanting to see all problems as blockades rather than seeing problems for what they are and then figuring out solutions. Rather than living in the negativity of constant fear or worries, taking control of your optimistic mindset also brings a better connection with colleagues, teammates, partners, bosses, and others. Empathy is an important tool in business, too, because we have to rely on other people for a variety of things. People want to do good work for/with those who are appreciative of their efforts and opinions.

COULD SOME STRESS BE GOOD?

It may seem hard to imagine, but there's research that shows how a certain amount of stress can help us perform and push us to excel. You've probably experienced that fine line between excitement and stress. Or maybe you've had a situation that was a little stressful but it forced you to step up to the plate and make a much needed change—and then all is well.

IT'S SCIENCE!

Melanie Greenberg, PhD, says, "Some researchers suggest that exposure to a moderate level of stress that you can master, can actually make you stronger and better able to manage stress, just like a vaccine, which contains a tiny amount of the bug, can immunize you against getting the disease. Richard Dienstbier's (1989) theory of mental toughness suggests that experiencing some manageable stressors, with recovery in between, can make us more mentally/physically tough and less reactive to future stress."[23]

I can pick out a few business experiences that were stressful but that also pushed me to rise to the occasion. I enjoyed the excitement of proposing a bold, private-label project and having the client say yes before I had fully figured out all the logistics. (Private label is when you make a product for another brand under their name, like when we produced our product for companies such as Estee Lauder, Bath & Body Works, or H2O PLUS.) But knowing that I *had* an order gave me the determination to get to it and find the best solutions. It was exciting but nerve-wracking, in a good way. Good stress can also come in the form of a promotion at work where you're super excited about the new position, the new opportunities, and higher pay but likely have some anxiety about expectations and ability. Your mindset and breath are a guiding force during times of the good stress, too.

In fact, as I write this book I'm experiencing what I'd consider to be good stress. I'm grateful to have turned my idea into a book proposal and gotten a publisher, but I'm on a much shorter than usual timeframe for writing. My whole heart is in this, and there's a bit of stress in wondering if this will be everything I've visualized it to be. Here's hoping it turned out well!

Watch your thoughts, they become words;

Watch your words, they become actions;

Watch your actions, they become habits;

Watch your habits, they become character;

Watch your character, for it becomes your destiny.

LAO TZU

3

BREATHE YOUR
GOALS TO LIFE

One conscious breath in and out is a meditation.
—ECKHART TOLLE

Back in the days following my Savasana breakthrough, I was completely intrigued about what else I could "make happen" with my breath. I was beginning to master the five minutes of empowering stillness in class, so I decided to take the magic of 3DB off my yoga mat and into my office. It has been the most powerful tool in my entrepreneurial tool kit ever since. Because I had no business experience and often felt unqualified to do things that I dreamed of doing in business, breath always made me feel like "I could." It became clear that breath, like many other things in life, has a basic version and upgraded versions. Whenever possible, it's nice to experience an upgrade, right? So, I continued to experiment with intentional breaths to help connect my mind and body and access a more patient, focused, confident, and successful version of myself.

UPGRADE YOUR BREATH

Your shallow, automated breath is simply your basic "factory setting" version. It does what it's supposed to do, but it's capable of delivering so much more . . . if you're willing to change the setting. The great thing about upgrading the breath is that there's no extra fee. It's simply a decision that you make. As you get to know the power of your breath, you'll see that it has many different applications; it's a tool for taking preventive measures as well as healing, restoring, supporting, empowering, and transforming.

> *If only I could bottle upgraded breath! I'd have longer lines than Starbucks in the morning. When we can buy a solution to feel better, we all want it, but when it requires a little effort and it's free, it may seem less coveted. Trust me, the power of upgraded breath is priceless. We can't afford not to upgrade.*

I began my experimentation with breath in business with the one tool that is still my go-to favorite: 3DB. It could not be simpler. 3DB at key moments gave me the strength to take leaps, see things more clearly, and make mindful decisions. I also began to experiment more on my yoga mat during class to see the difference that came from focusing on breath rather than the yoga poses. I began to have a new level of clarity and creativity during yoga class. Using different breaths throughout class cleared my head and made me *feel* better. In addition, some of my most creative ideas came shortly after I had been doing deep breathing. It's the breath that has kept me coming back to class for almost thirty years now.

But breath doesn't have to be attached to movement to work its magic. Bringing breath into business helped manage my negative emotions by letting them go with each deep exhale and bringing in confidence, optimism, and a higher level of patience with each inhale. I felt stronger emotionally as I built my business. My body also benefited; I had a new sense of physical energy from believing that I *could*. I was able to achieve milestones faster than I had imagined.

CUSTOMIZING BREATH WITH MULTIPLIERS (EYES CLOSED, VISUALIZATION, MANTRAS, INTENTIONS) FOR YOUR OWN UNIQUE MIX OF EMPOWERMENT

It didn't take long before I was using a variety of breath techniques and experimenting with different combinations of positive thoughts, intentions, visualizations, and mantras with each new type of breath that I learned. It was clear that my standard shallow breath wouldn't help when we received defective products from our manufacturer and our biggest client was already out of stock, but *alternate nostril breathing* could bring me back into balance to handle the crisis. Shallow, automatic breath wouldn't help when I had to negotiate price with a big client, but *breath retention* exercises helped me learn to move through discomfort in order to find something better. Shallow breath was no help at all when I was told "no" at critical steps along the journey, but *lion's breath* allowed me to immediately let go of that "no" physically and find a better match for whatever I needed.

IT'S SCIENCE!

Integrative Breathwork Facilitator John Luckovich says, "The chronic stress that is associated with shallow breathing results in lower amounts of lymphocyte, a type of white blood cell that helps to defend the body from invading organisms, and lowers the amounts of proteins that signal other immune cells. The body is then susceptible to contracting acute illnesses, aggravating preexisting medical conditions, and prolonging healing times."[24]

I'll be sharing my top six breathing techniques in this chapter. There are many more techniques, but for the purpose of introducing you to the power of breath, I'm sticking with my favorites—which also happen to be simple, fast, and effective. You may find that these breaths can be a gateway to longer meditations or other types of breath techniques. High-five if you do. Or you may find that you like only *one* type of enhanced breath . . . forever. High-five there, too; one new breath can be completely game changing! The beauty of breath and using it as a vehicle to connect the mind and body is that there are endless ways to keep it unique to you by adding any of the multipliers (closed eyes, positive thoughts, mantras, visualization) to any of the different breaths mentioned here or other techniques that you learn elsewhere. You can keep it simple or get more creative, but it'll always feel fresh because every day is a new experience.

NO INCENSE, NO HOLDING HANDS, NO CHANTING

I have a business sensibility about breath and meditation. Although my journey into breath came directly from yoga, my breath practice has always been very functional. No incense. No Sanskrit chants. No crystals. No trying to reach total enlightenment. Just you and your breath are necessary to take full advantage of the science behind changing your breath, managing your emotions, and accessing your maximum potential. Making breath a "spiritual" practice is wonderful, but don't let the idea of that hold you back. It's all within you, available anytime, anywhere, free refills included. Just you and your breath.

Breathing may be one of those things that you don't need to fully understand or even believe in for it to work. So even if you don't think the practice will do much to calm your brain, give it a try— it probably will help you in spite of yourself.

— ALICE G. WALTON, PhD, BIOPSYCHOLOGY AND BEHAVIORAL NEUROSCIENCE[25]

My Top Six Breathing Techniques:

1. 3DB (three deep breaths)

2. Lion's breath

3. Alternate nostril breathing

4. Ujjayi

5. Breath retention

6. Bumble bee breath

Breath practice in Sanskrit is called *pranayama*. "Prana" means breath or life force, and "yama" means to control. I've found that through my breath practice, a specific breath can have the power to offer different outcomes in different situations. For example, some people use the lavender plant to calm themselves in their evening bath, whereas others use lavender aromatherapy to energize their spirit. I can take 3DB in situations when I need to calm my nerves, but in other cases, those 3DB will energize me. The main difference for me is what I'm thinking. Attaching thoughts to the breath will inform the body. Remember the power of your mind and see how different breaths can have more than one result.

THE IMPORTANCE OF NASAL BREATHING

In yoga, we breathe in and out through our nose unless we're doing a specific breath that's designed to exhale through the mouth, like lion's breath (explained in a moment).

IT'S SCIENCE!

Northwestern University's Feinberg School of Medicine Assistant professor of neurology Christina Zelano confirms that "Inhaling through the nose stimulates the brain. Doing so through the mouth however causes little stimulation." The article also states that "The Northwestern team delved further and found that three major areas of the brain are affected by breathing: the hippocampus which is responsible for memory, the amygdala—our emotional center, and the piriform cortex, which controls our olfactory system or our sense of smell."[26]

Whenever possible during these breathing techniques, inhale and exhale through your nose unless you're doing a breath specifically designed to use your mouth, such as lion's breath.

> *The science of breathing stands on quite ancient foundations. Centuries of wisdom instructs us to pay closer attention to our breathing, the most basic of things we do each day. And yet, maybe because breathing is so basic, it's also easy to ignore. A brief review of the latest science on breathing and the brain, and overall health, serves as a reminder that breathing deserves much closer attention —there's more going on with each breath than we realize.*

— DAVID DISALVO, author of *Brain Changer: How Harnessing Your Brain's Power to Adapt Can Change Your Life*[27]

LET'S BREATHE: MY TOP SIX BREATH EXERCISES

Try one at a time and get to know the power of your breath better with each exercise. Experiment with the exercises in different situations. Mix and match. Make them your own. If you're not feeling it with one method, you can always come back to it at a later time when it may resonate more.

It's Science!

According to Harvard Health Publishing: "Deep breathing also goes by the names diaphragmatic breathing, abdominal breathing, belly breathing. . . . When you breathe deeply, air coming in through your nose fully fills your lungs, and the lower belly rises. For many, deep breathing seems unnatural . . . body image has a negative impact on respiration in our culture. This interferes with deep breathing and gradually makes shallow 'chest breathing' seem normal, which increases tension and anxiety . . . and limits the diaphragm's range of motion."[28]

3DB (THREE DEEP BREATHS)

Just looking at those words (three deep breaths) makes me happy. 3DB have served as a gateway to experiencing an inner strength and control that I had no idea I could access. It doesn't get easier than this. The more frequently you take your 3DB, the more your body will crave them and automatically remind you to take them sooner rather than later. It's almost like there's exponential power with each of the 3DB. They can change your emotions, state of mind, and perspective in under a minute. To achieve the full benefits of deep breathing, try to not just breathe deeply into your chest but to expand your belly on the inhale. Think about the way babies breathe, how their tummy really expands before their chest. It feels counter-intuitive to adults, but keep it in mind. Every deep breath feels good, but you can maximize it with your diaphragm rather than your chest.

Let's Breathe

With these three deep breaths, inhale and exhale through your nose. Make an effort to lengthen your inhales so that you feel full of breath and expansion in your belly, and then exhale fully until you feel empty of the breath. You can place a hand on your belly to get to know the feeling of expanded deep breath. On the inhale, your belly will expand and, on the exhale, it contracts. It can feel counterintuitive; it just takes practice. No expectations—just experience it. Get to know your breath a little bit. With each time that you repeat this, begin to *feel* it. Close your eyes and go inward. Maybe even smile; it'll make you feel happy. If 3DB lead to four or five, that's fine, too. If you were comfortable with one or two right now, that's a start.

Hold tight to the idea that 3DB are always with you. You have to ability to immediately regroup and refocus in under sixty seconds. 3DB are packed with power to make a big shift in real time so that you can make mindful decisions and work with a positive and clear energy. Consider yourself armed and positive!

3DB to the Rescue

I distinctly remember the first panic attack I ever had. I was walking around the fabric district in downtown Los Angeles. I spent quite a bit of time there in the startup days, because before we were able to print our own fabric, I had to buy rolls of already printed fabrics from small fabric shops. As my business grew, I had gotten to know many of the store owners as I straddled the uncomfortable place between not having enough of these overrun fabric rolls and not yet being big enough for the minimum quantity requirements to design and print our own custom-designed fabric. I felt overwhelmed with frustration as I was downtown one day. I got dizzy and began to sweat; my heart was racing and I felt like I was going to faint. I had never experienced a panic attack. I went into one of the stores and sat down to take some slow, deep breaths and regroup. I added in some positive thoughts and felt my body soaking them in. Not only did the breaths make me feel better, but they turned this painful situation into a milestone moment; I was able to see that I was so stressed and anxious about the ongoing issue that something had to give.

I decided that it was time to negotiate with a local fabric printing company and take the leap of faith to design and print our own custom fabrics. That was it. After a year of several visits to the fabric district every week, I bid farewell to the small store owners and began to design and print our own fabrics. The panic attack turned out to be a blessing in disguise, and it reinforced my appreciation for breath to bring strength and relief, allowing me to regroup and refocus to make a much needed yet very intimidating change.

LION'S BREATH

Everyone over the age of three should know, love, and use lion's breath. It may look silly, but you usually do it when you're alone, so who cares? I taught this to my kids when they were young because it was a fun way for them to physically let go of a bad feeling. It's a healthy tool since it's difficult to explain emotional behavior to a three-year-old. Not only does it work in the sandbox, but it's just as effective in the office, too. Lion's breath relieves tension and is an energizing and cleansing breath. Not much scientific validation is required here; you'll quickly see that it just feels so darn good and is an immediate release of tension and stress as it brings a new sense of confidence. It has to be done fiercely like a lion for its full effect! Try three in a row.

Let's Breathe

Take a really deep inhale with your eyes closed; on the exhale, simultaneously stick out your tongue with fervor and sigh out all negativity while opening your eyes as wide as you can. Occasionally, I add a shaking out of my hands because I tend to hold stress in my hands. Although the hand-shaking part is not the traditional style of lion's breath, this shows the fun of customizing breath for what works best for you to feel good. This breath often leads to a giggle afterward, but there's nothing funny about how incredibly liberating and fierce (like a lion) it feels! It also tends to free up a tension-clenched jaw. I dare you to *not* enjoy lion's breath. Lion's breath can be like an exorcising because you can energetically let something out of your system. Your tongue dispels the negative thoughts or energy. It's immediately freeing. Maybe we should have a #LionsBreath Instagram photo contest!

ALTERNATE NOSTRIL BREATHING

This breath is a favorite because it balances the nervous system, and makes you feel grounded and strong. It's a great option before an important meeting, before giving a presentation, or when you are having a difficult conversation. Whatever the case may be, it takes just a few cycles of this balancing breath to feel more centered and focused. It activates the parasympathetic nervous system (the "rest and digest" system) and makes you feel as though you've got your act together. Alternate nostril breathing brings harmony to the left and right sides of your brain. Breathing in through your left nostril accesses the right side of your brain (the creative side), and breathing in through your right nostril accesses your left brain (the analytical/logical side). We don't breathe equally through each nostril at all times. One side may be a little more clogged than the other, and it switches up periodically throughout the day. Alternate nostril breathing can help us feel some equanimity.

Let's Breathe

Sit up tall. Close your eyes. Take your dominant hand and rest your thumb on one nostril and your ring finger on the other nostril. Your index and middle finger can rest on your forehead and your pinky is just along for the ride, in the air. These instructions are for the right-handed. Lefty friends: just swap the words right and left in these instructions.

1. Close the right nostril with your right thumb and inhale through the left nostril.

2. Close the left nostril with the right hand's ring finger and release the right thumb.

3. Exhale through the right nostril, keeping the left nostril closed.

4. Inhale through the right nostril; close it with the thumb.

5. Release the ring finger from the left side and exhale through the left nostril.

6. Repeat the full cycles for a few rounds of right/left.

UJJAYI BREATH

This is a classic yoga breath also known as whispering, ocean, or victorious breath. Ujjayi breath is usually done while moving through yoga poses to generate heat internally, but I find it helpful on its own, too. It feels as if you're revving up your internal engine, and the sound helps to make you feel present. It's detoxifying and can help regulate blood pressure. It helps to slow the breath and calm the nerves. It improves focus and clarity with just a few rounds. Melissa Eisler (via Chopra.com) describes ujjayi breath as "having a balancing influence on the entire cardiorespiratory system" and it "releases feelings of irritation and frustration, and helps calm the mind and body." She lists the benefits as follows:

- Increases the amount of oxygen in the blood

- Builds internal body heat

- Relieves tension

- Encourages free flow of prana

- Builds energy

- Detoxifies mind and body

- Increases feelings of presence, self-awareness, and meditative qualities[29]

Let's Breathe

Ujjayi is always done through the nose only:

1. Inhale through your nose and exhale slowly as if you're trying to fog up a mirror (except your mouth is closed). The sound comes from initiating a slight contraction at the back of your throat for a long "haaaa" sound.

2. Take a long, slow inhale, and on the exhale, direct the breath slowly across the back of your throat to re-create that "haaaa" sound.

3. Repeat a few times. It quickly becomes rhythmic and energizing.

I love using ujjayi when I need to clear my head and get back to the "blank canvas" in my mind, like taking a walk, putting my earbuds in, and instead of turning anything on, listening to my ujjayi breath and clearing my mind. It's detoxifying and brings a calm yet strong energy.

BREATH RETENTION

Breath retention, of course, means holding your breath. That hold can be done after an inhale or an exhale. There are numerous ways to integrate breath retention. For me, breath retention is analogous for seeing that being uncomfortable can lead to something better. When we hold our inhale and get to the point right before we absolutely have to exhale, it can feel uncomfortable and for me a bit claustrophobic as well. It's an exercise that helps me realize that when I push my boundaries it's not enjoyable in the moment but leads to growth and, in the case of breath, leads to a release of tension. Breath retention is known for restoring energy, increasing alertness, detoxing the respiratory system, and even boosting immunity. It also helps you get present as you focus exclusively on your breath.

Let's Breathe

When we inhale, we're bringing in oxygen. On the exhale we are letting out carbon dioxide, which helps to detoxify our body. Seventy percent of our toxins are let out through our exhales with the carbon dioxide. As you practice breath retention exercises over time, you can play with the length on all parts of the breath: inhales, exhales, and holds. Here's a general rule of thumb: When the exhales are longer than the inhales and the holds, it brings a calming feeling and your nervous systems slows down. When your inhales and exhales are the same length, it indicates balance and ease. There are so many different ways and levels to practice breath retention, so we'll ease into the idea of breath retention with this simple yet effective calming version:

1. Inhales and exhales are through the nose.

2. Breath in for a count of 4.

3. Exhale for a count of 6–8.

4. Inhale for a count of 4.

5. Exhale for a count of 6–8.

6. Repeat 3–4 times to bring on relaxation.

BUMBLE BEE OR BEE BREATH

No epi pen required; nobody's allergic to bee breath! This simple and fun technique will have you buzzing in no time. It's energizing and clearing. It helps concentration and memory, and I love to do it to clear my monkey mind and make room for creativity and clarity. This breath makes a noise as you hum on the exhale, so pick the right location when you do this one. It's not a very common breathing technique, but I've loved it from the first time I learned it because anything that can clear my head so quickly is a winner. Thanks, Christina Holmes!

Let's Breathe

Take a seat. Shoulders up and back. Start by closing your eyes and taking a deep breath. Inhales and exhales are through the nose. Raise both hands, palms facing you at the height of your eyes. Place each thumb on the cartilage of your ear (left thumb on left ear, right thumb on right ear) and gently press it closed. Put the rest of your fingers over each of your eyes. So, all four fingers of each hand are covering each eye and the thumb is gently closing the ear. Take a long inhale through your nose, and as you exhale, make a humming sound—hmmm. It should sound like a bee is buzzing right next to your ear. Continue exhaling until you are empty of oxygen. Then repeat for 3–5 cycles. Your mind should feel clear and energized. Now go get creative and productive!

As you begin to try different kinds of breath, you'll see what feels right for certain times of day or specific scenarios. You can begin to mix and match breath techniques with the multipliers (eyes closed, positive intention, mantra, visualization) however you'd like. It's kind of like how we thoughtfully choose our food at each meal based on what makes us feel best (vegan, organic, non-GMO, paleo, keto, non-dairy, etc.). It's time that we also order up some healthy emotions a few times a day, too. There's a veritable buffet of breath and mindset combinations—something for everyone! Here are some of my favorite "Breath for Success Recipes" to give you some ideas for customizing.

BREATH FOR SUCCESS RECIPES

If you make soup a lot like I do, you know that most soups start with the same three ingredients (chopped onions, celery, and carrot). But then you get creative and add all sorts of vegetables and spices and that's what makes each soup very different. Many breath and mindfulness techniques also start with foundational ingredients: breath, closed eyes, and positive intentions and/or mantra, but what makes them feel unique each time is the combination of breath along with different thoughts and intentions. As with vegetable soup, many people still appreciate recipes for guidance, so I've developed these breath recipes. Rest assured that you can't go wrong when you mix in a variety of things that you enjoy. Use your creativity in developing mantras and intentions with different breath styles, and each time you breathe it'll always feel a little different because the elements or situation has changed in some way. Practicing a variety of these techniques daily will help to significantly lower the production of the stress hormone cortisol, increase attention and focus, create the ability to be present in the moment, and improve deep sleep.

WAKE UP! SWAP ANXIETY FOR POSITIVITY

Waking up and immediately feeling anxious is not a good way to start the day. Whether you have had a bad night's sleep, have been carrying a lot of worry and anxiety, or have a nerve-wracking business day ahead of you, it's important to take control right away. Before leaving your bed, sit up and swap the negative energy for positive intention and inner strength. It can change the trajectory of your day immediately. You'll feel empowered.

Ingredients: *Three deep breaths, eyes closed, positive thought (optional)*

Recipe: *Sit up tall and in a position that feels strong and confident. Close your eyes. With each deep breath, mentally acknowledge that you're inhaling fresh oxygen and happily send out negative energy with each long, slow exhale. Taking that mental energy swap first thing never disappoints. It's like an espresso for your mind; I call it "Breathspresso." Breath alone can work its magic, but if you want to add a positive thought to replace any negative thoughts, do it. Good morning!*

"GUT INSTINCT" TUNE-UP

Having strong gut instincts is important in business since you have to make quick decisions frequently. When you can trust your gut and your initial instincts, you make better decisions. Occasionally, though, we feel as if we've lost that connection. Maybe you've gotten into a rut where bad decisions find you in a place where you don't want to be. So now you'll second-guess your gut instinct. Remember the "Seinfeld" episode where George Costanza feels like this and decides to go with the opposite of what he'd normally do? Instead of doing that, get back in touch with your gut instinct. It's an important connection for decision making.

Ingredients: *Three deep breaths, eyes closed, hands on belly, intention to reset your connection to gut instinct*

Recipe: *Lying down or sitting up, place both hands on your belly. Close your eyes and visualize energy flowing from your breath and tapping into your gut instinct with each inhale, reconnecting your mind and body. With each exhale, let go of any negative emotions or lack of confidence. Complete at least 3DB while consciously thinking about being able to trust your gut again. This method of placing your hands where you want to send your breath to deepen your connection can also work with your throat and eyes to feel more connected to your truth or your vision. For example, if you're having trouble speaking your truth or can't seem to communicate the way you want to, take a few deep breaths with your hands gently on your throat and chest area and consciously breathe some fresh energy into the area of your throat. Or cover your eyes gently and breathe into your eyes,*

connecting to your inner "vision" or opening up the
energy to see things in a new or clearer way. Just
sending some breath into a specific part of your body
can open your mind to the idea of unlocking the stag-
nant energy. That's as woo-woo as I get, but it works!

TURNING REJECTION INTO MOMENTUM

Rejection is an inevitable part of business, but we often take it personally. Instead, you can use rejection as "fuel for your fire." It can make you feel more determined if you decide to look at it as momentum. Sure, take a minute to acknowledge that you're disappointed, and then let your breath immediately shift your perspective, knowing that you will find a better opportunity or solution. Every "no" can lead to a better "yes"! "No" is not the enemy; it simply leads to another way. Looking back in my business life, I see many rejections that led to something so much better. Hindsight is 20/20, so take rejection with a better attitude rather than letting it set you back.

Ingredients: *Lion's breath, positive mantra (optional)*

Recipe: *Immediately, as you experience rejection and could easily begin to steep in the dark mood that comes along with it, turn to your lion's breath to let it go. Stand up tall, shoulders up and back. Take a deep inhale with your eyes closed; on the exhale,*

*simultaneously stick out your tongue and open your
eyes as wide as you can. Make a sighing sound. If you
feel like adding in some words of wisdom (something
like "I am focused and persistent and will not quit")
to give you some inner strength, go ahead! Otherwise,
the lion's breath alone can dispel the negative energy
and convert it to momentum and determination.
Repeat lion's breath three times and move on with
fierce energy.*

MOVE OVER, MONKEY MIND; MAKE ROOM FOR CREATIVITY AND CLARITY

Creativity comes from a clear mind that feels like it
has room to expand. When our mind feels like it's running in circles and there's just too much happening in
our brains, we need to clear out and start with a clean
slate. It's like opening a window, letting the stale air
out, hearing the birds chirp (and the bees hum!), and
bringing in a fresh, clear energy to start anew. Clarity is
important in both your intention setting as well as your
communication. In an article titled "Clarity: Your First
Priority," Success.com columnist and author Tony Jeary
defines clarity in business as follows: "From a leadership
perspective, clarity means having an unfettered view of
your vision, which is what you want and why you want
it, fed by an understanding of its purpose and value. In

the old days, executives didn't see any need to explain the why. They simply expected people to fall in line and do what they were told. But when people understand the why of things (the purpose and value), the combination produces a level of clarity that has enough influence or pull to actually become motivational. It becomes the fuel of voluntary change that enables you to be pulled toward your vision, rather than pushed."[30] Having clarity allows you to move forward and take action from a place of strength and confidence. Breathe into clarity and creativity.

Ingredients: *Bumble bee breath, closed eyes*

Recipe: *Take a seat. Shoulders up and back. Start by closing your eyes and taking a deep breath. Inhales and exhales are through the nose. Raise both hands, palms facing you at the height of your eyes. Place each thumb on the cartilage of your ear (left thumb on left ear, right thumb on right ear) and gently press it closed. Put the rest of your fingers over each of your eyes. So, all four fingers of each hand are covering each eye and the thumb is gently closing the ear. Take a long inhale through your nose, and as you exhale, make a humming sound, similar to a buzzing bee. Continue exhaling until you are empty of oxygen. Repeat for 3–5 cycles as you completely clear your head and make abundant space for clarity and creativity.*

GRATITUDE IS THE BEST ATTITUDE

> *The more you are grateful for what you have,*
> *the more you will have to be grateful for.*
> — ZIG ZIGLER

Along with breath, focusing on gratitude is always a winning strategy in business and life. When I'm feeling as if I want to focus on only what's missing, this thought brings me back to being appreciative of all the achievements that I've already accomplished. The mental adjustment is enough to completely change your energy into positivity. If you're going through a difficult business situation, move your attention away from what's *not* happening, or what you're *not* getting, and focus on the positive aspects of your work that you actually have. Be grateful for the fact that you *have* your own business, or that you enjoy your work and your colleagues, or that this challenge will lead to something bigger and better.

IT'S SCIENCE!

According to psychologist Randy Kamen, "What we have learned is that cultivating personal attributes fortifies us during times of adversity and emotional turmoil and leads to greater happiness and resilience. Moreover, of all the attributes one can develop, gratitude is most strongly associated with mental health. Being grateful also impacts the overall experience of happiness, and these effects tend to be long-lasting."[31]

Ingredients: *3DB, three things you're grateful for, journal (optional)*

Recipe: *Think of three things that you're grateful for today. Lying down or sitting cross legged, take 3DB, and with each inhale, silently recite one thing that you're grateful for. On the exhale, release any tension. If you want to stick with one thing for all 3DB, that's fine too. Writing in a gratitude journal is a powerful exercise. You might want to grab a journal and begin to repeat this exercise daily while writing down your gratitude list. Shifting into gratitude has brought tremendous rewards to my business life. It took self-awareness to see that I frequently tended to focus on what I needed to get next—always in a cycle of thought about what was missing and how I could get it. Becoming disciplined and making gratitude my new default made a huge difference. The shift in perspective really works.*

BUH-BYE TENSION, I'M COOL AS A CUCUMBER

Who doesn't like to feel balanced, patient, grounded, strong, and in charge? I'll take this any day. When you need to get rid of tension or anxiety and get back to feeling cool as a cucumber, alternate nostril breathing always delivers.

Ingredients: *Alternate nostril breathing, closed eyes, positive mantra (optional)*

Recipe:

1. *Close the right nostril with your right thumb and inhale through the left nostril.*

2. *Close the left nostril with the right hand's ring finger and release the right thumb.*

3. *Exhale through the right nostril, keeping the left nostril closed.*

4. *Inhale through the right nostril; close it with the thumb.*

5. *Release the ring finger from the left side and exhale through the left nostril.*

6. *Repeat the full cycles for a few rounds of right/left.*

I usually do alternate nostril breathing without a mantra because I'm focused on the opening and closing of the nostrils and visualizing my breath. But if you need to have a thought to focus on in order to change your state of mind, try experimenting with it.

This is where the fun begins . . . You're now empowered with the knowledge of how your breath and mind work together in controlling your thoughts, emotion, and energy. You can mix and match any of the breath techniques and multipliers as ready. You don't have to wait for a challenge or annoying situation; the more you want to indulge in enhanced breathing, the better. Begin to use it as simply a way to help you stay on track—a maintenance tool for inner strength and higher energy.

If you're not quite sure where to start, use the recipes to begin. If you're looking for a specific time or place to begin to make some changes, I bet you'll benefit from looking carefully at your digital lifestyle habits (Chapter 4) or your morning routine (Chapter 5).

4

DIGITAL WELLNESS:
UNPLUG TO RECHARGE

*Almost everything will work again if you unplug
it for a few minutes . . . including you.*
—ANNE LAMOTT

Tech has revolutionized the business sector, and you're likely feeling the effects of less humanity and more technology. Of course, tech and business go hand in hand, so I'd be remiss if I didn't include the subject of digital wellness. So many of us are feeling the effects of constantly connected business life. Working at the pace of technology is not sustainable. Mindful breathing is the antidote. Science is showing that our cognitive and social behaviors are negatively affected by our habitual screen time. In some cases, our devices are controlling our lives. We've developed unconscious reflexive habits, and sometimes they can occur dozens or even hundreds of times every day. I'm familiar with experiencing a false sense of productivity from my reflexive check-ins on everything from email to texts to banking, social, and news feeds. I was by far more distracted than productive. We're connected more than we're not. There are less chunks of time for getting into the creative zone and too much bobbing and weaving with multitasking.

IT'S SCIENCE!

Neurologist Richard E. Cytowic says, "In terms of energy use, switching attention incurs a high cost. We are not good at it. Our brains still operate at speeds of about 120 bits (~15 bytes) per second. It takes roughly sixty bits per second to pay attention to one person speaking, half our allotment right there. Arithmetic shows why multitasking degrades performance. Verizon's fiber optic connection shoots data into my home at 5,000 times the rate my biological brain can handle."[32]

That's crazy fast. We've hit the tipping point of living in the fast lane. It's time for a market correction, a recalibration for our digital wellness. Don't sacrifice your human life for digital life. You can't live at the speed of wireless data. Of course, I'm not saying that we need to completely rebel; I'm just suggesting that we should go for a more strategic and conscious connection with our screens. Manoush Zomorodi, an expert on the human relationship with tech, jokes in her TEDX talk, "A UX designer astutely pointed out during one of our conversations that the only people who refer to their customers as 'users' are drug dealers—and technologists."[33] Uh-oh. It's no mistake that we are literally feeling drawn to our screens way more than necessary. Let this chapter serve as your friendly digital intervention (should you need one). Take a deep breath for a moment.

Close your eyes and think about your digital habits:

- Should you consider being more structured with your connected lifestyle?

- Is your connected business lifestyle getting in the way of your productivity? Creativity? Time management?

- Has your attachment to constantly checking email or apps become a vicious cycle of mental fatigue?

- Have you lost a little control of your time, energy, and positivity?

- When was the last time you consciously unplugged to literally rest your brain and clear your mind?

Did you surprise yourself with any of those answers? I didn't realize the extent of my digital attachment and distraction until both of my sons pointed it out—at different times, more than once. And they were teenagers. It seems that most of us could likely use tweaks in this department. The long-term effect of our connected lives isn't yet fully understood, but medical experts and scientists have been talking about the impact of technology on our health for several years already and it's been falling on deaf ears. We may not have been ready to listen yet, but we're getting there. It's reminiscent of the 1960s and '70s, when smoking was found to be dangerous for our health but people didn't (or wouldn't) listen because they enjoyed smoking and were likely addicted. What's old is new again.

RESPECTING OUR BRAIN

Eyeballs are the new currency; we are living in the "attention economy." Brands want our attention and we have to sift through emails, ads and notifications to figure out what's worth our time and effort. The vetting can be exhausting and unproductive. Deciding where your attention goes is an important decision that you make over and over all day long. Those decisions can quickly add up to situations that you won't like to find yourself in: running late, not doing your best quality work, and not able to fully tap into your creativity or focus. Our brain wasn't made for the extremes that we subject it to in the form of screen time, multitasking, and distractions. Some negative side effects of round-the-clock connection are interrupted sleep patterns, taking attention away from real-life engagement, anxiety, depression, posture issues, brain fog, and decreased productivity. It's not all rainbows and butterflies as we live life in front of our screens. Digital life can feel depleting. Until it's not! You can *choose* to stop the madness once you become self-aware of your tendencies. You are in charge of your digital decisions. Your brain probably needs more Savasana, right?

IT'S SCIENCE!

Loren Frank, assistant professor in the Department of Physiology at the University of California San Francisco, specializes in learning and memory. According to Frank, "Like other muscles in our body, the brain needs time to recover from constant stimulation. Almost certainly, downtime lets the brain go over experiences it's had, solidify them and turn them into permanent long-term memories. When the brain is constantly stimulated you prevent this learning process."[34]

We haven't ever had to think about how our brain might be feeling until now. Let's begin to give our brain the same respect and downtime that we give a sore back or overworked abs. Since we don't have the same physical "soreness" from our brain, we have to instead get mindful about noticing mental fatigue, brain fog, and other symptoms of digital overload such as impatience, sleep deprivation, and isolation.

Just as you applied self-awareness to take a good look at your negative thought patterns and emotional habits, self-awareness comes into play to assess your cognitive function and level of, let's say, digital discontent. Business goes much more smoothly when your mind is clear and energized. Chances are that you spend more time than you think connected and/or distracted. The good news is that once you become aware of which digital habits are holding you back, you can interrupt that behavior and *Breathe Like a Boss* to stop, get quiet, reorganize, and recharge. Even for little bits of time, it makes an impactful difference. Consciously think about resting your brain while you take some deep breaths, and you'll begin to see the brain fog clear out.

CHALLENGE YOURSELF WITH ONE SWAP THIS WEEK

I began making a small digital shift by challenging myself for a week to call a client or business colleague instead of emailing. Even for a simple business issue, pick up the phone to place the order, ask the question, confirm the answer. I started with my printer and realized that it may have been a year since I spoke with him last, and I adore my printer. Things can easily become transactional via email. The "Hope you're doing well" salutation doesn't come close to asking and listening. It was eye-opening because I realized that I had built up a dislike for talking on the phone because it's time consuming and it can feel awkward and bothersome; you don't know what the person is doing when you call, and, well, email is faster and feels efficient. That's where we've headed—away from connection and conversation and toward transactional behavior. When I hung up the phone each time, I was literally smiling. Lesson learned.

Email doesn't nurture relationships, and in some cases, it can hinder a situation because things don't always translate well via email. Human connection can reduce the risk of misinterpretation and misunderstanding that could cost you business. A *New York Times* article about Google's Mindfulness program–turned-book called *Search Inside Yourself*, developed by former Google engineer Chade-Meng Tan (more on Tan in Chapter 6), mentions this very issue. Writer Caitlin Kelly says, "One of its tenets is mindful e-mailing. Mr. Tan says it's too easy to focus on the message we're sending, and not on its recipients and the possible impact on them. When recipients don't know the intent behind the email—as is often the case—they tend to assume the worst, like anger or frustration on the sender's part. Tans says, 'We frequently get offended or frightened by emails that were never intended to offend or frighten. If we are emotionally unskillful, then we react with offense or fear, and then all hell breaks loose.'"[35]

Nurturing relationships is a big part of success in business, and it requires effort. Think about picking up the phone a few more times every week. It's refreshing. Back to basics feels good. I've seen the value of talking and the value of "pounding the pavement" firsthand since I launched my business, before our lives became fully immersed in tech. I literally pounded the pavement in search of manufacturing in the garment district in Los Angeles. Now, every resource is at our fingertips, but it's not quite the same. It's wonderful in a different way, but talking with people, meeting with people, seeing things in person makes a world of difference even if only on occasion now. It can be inspiring and can lead to new opportunities too. That little challenge turned into a whole new perspective that lasted way beyond that week. What can you challenge yourself with this week to lessen your digital connection and deepen your human connection in even some small way?

IT'S NOT JUST THE YOUNG'UNS

If you assume that digital addiction applies only to millennials, you'd be wrong. Data show that it's the Gen X'ers (born in the early-to-mid 1960s to the early 1980s) who can't seem to separate from tech. That's me in there. Social media engagement, digital marketing, email, customer relationship management, and sales and cash flow are all key elements of business that keep us constantly connected for up-to-the-minute status. But would it really kill us to peek only, say, three times a day instead of dozens? And speaking of that, you might want to consider scheduling your email checks when you're in a strong state of mind, because the act of reading emails can be stress inducing for many people. Have you heard of "email apnea"? It's holding your breath while checking email. Do you subconsciously do this? Alex Soojung-Kim Pang Pang, a researcher at the Institute for the Future, a Silicon Valley think tank, and author of *The Distraction Addiction*, explains: "This reflects the anxiety many of us feel as we check for new messages in our inbox, not knowing what new fires we'll have to put out or what problems we'll have to solve. Connection is inevitable. Distraction is a choice."[36] Choose wisely. If you're checking email frequently, that means you could be subjecting yourself to a constant low-grade state of stress.

It's Science!

Josh Axe, certified doctor of natural medicine, doctor of chiropractic, and clinical nutritionist, says, "You may think that it's necessary to work under the gun all of the time, but according to the University of Maryland Medical Center, chronic stress affects your ability to concentrate, act efficiently and makes you more accident-prone. Chronic stress has devastating effects on memory and learning. It actually kills brain cells. The Franklin Institute explains that the stress hormone cortisol channels glucose to the muscles during the stress response and leaves less fuel for the brain."[37]

As if that's not enough, chronic stress also affects many other systems of our body, including the heart, immunity, weight, pain, and aging. Breath is the antidote. The entrepreneurial journey and business as a whole is tough; in a very real sense, our journey is similar to professional athletes in the way that we frequently push our body and brain to the limit with exhaustion and stress. But athletes are super focused on their health and recovery from overexertion because it's their body (rather than their product or service) from which they derive success. We (the collective business sector) need to consider health, wellness, and recovery as a more integral part of success in business for ourselves, our teams, our colleagues, and employees as well. We need to commit to spending time recovering from tech by unplugging to recharge—and reconnecting with ourselves and one another. The more you begin to unplug in small increments, the better you'll feel. Don't look at it as punishment to be away from your screen; consider it like you would a workout or having a healthy meal. It's a much needed part of your wellness routine that always leaves you feeling better.

As you begin to see how energizing it feels to step away from your screens and begin to treat your brain like the muscle that it is, you'll probably begin to schedule longer chunks of disconnected time—even if you can't imagine that right now. Would you consider not checking your smartphone while you take a ten-minute walk outside or meet a friend for coffee? Rather than holding your phone, could you possibly put it in an unreachable distance away or actually turn it off whenever you're with someone to whom you should be paying full attention? Could you charge your phone at night in a room other than your bedroom or bathroom? The more you do these little hacks, the easier it becomes to experience little digital detox breaks. And believe it or not, the more protective you'll become of your energy and the more strategic you'll become in figuring out your new balance. If you need a structured program, journalist Catherine Price wrote an insightful book titled *How to Break Up with Your Phone: The 30-Day Plan to Take Back Your Life.*[38] It's chock-full of strategic advice to help you build a healthier relationship with your phone. Oh, and it's even more effective if you read the book while taking some deep breaths!

MY LOVE/HATE RELATIONSHIP WITH TECH

I've had an ongoing love/hate relationship with tech for many years. I've written about it, talked with friends and colleagues about it, and read lots of articles about it, and I had begun to admire people who were not attached to their screens—like my friend who frequently doesn't know where her phone is because she's not "digitally delinquent." She's in the moment most of the time—quite an aberration compared to almost everyone I know—and it's refreshing. I was the opposite. (I still can't imagine not knowing where my phone is . . . at least not yet.) I had an automatic reflex that kept me constantly connected, and it was exhausting. I was working harder, not smarter, and who wants to do that?

IT'S SCIENCE!

This point was bolstered a couple of years ago when I heard an inspiring talk by Dr. David Bach (Harvard-trained neurologist and founder of the Platypus Institute) on rewiring the brain to form healthy new habits. His entire talk had me riveted, and he closed with a point that really resonated, quoting Mark Twain: "It ain't what you don't know that hurts you. It's what you know for sure that just ain't so." I know, it takes a minute to latch on to that one. He slowly repeated it and then said, "One thing that many high achievers know *for sure* is that to be successful, you have to work harder than everyone else. In the world of rewiring in science, *that just ain't so*. When you rewire your unconscious mind, the new behavior becomes effortless and automatic like beating your heart. I encourage you to play with the notion that you can radically enhance your effectiveness with rewiring while working less hard and experiencing deep fulfillment."[39] Powerful, right? Especially in this scenario of digital overwhelm. Work smarter. Breathe better. Rewire your mind.

It took a little while, but I began to use my breath to rewire my brain and work smarter digitally. I slowly made progress, and the baby steps began to add up. Think about the amount of time that can add up if you are habitually connected to a screen, and yet it's not always attached to productivity. Depending on your habits, it very well may be a substantial amount of time. Can you imagine if you used that time instead to work on a passion project? Or a side gig that you've always said you don't have time to do? Or spend more time relaxing with a quiet mind that's open to your own new ideas? Use your deep breaths to give you inner strength to step away and reorganize. What would you want to do with that extra time that adds up over a week? A month? A year? Work toward rewiring your habits to make some extra time for *that*.

OVERCOMING FEELING NAKED WITHOUT MY PHONE

A couple of years ago, I wouldn't have dreamed of leaving the house without my smartphone. I wouldn't get more than one and a half steps out the door before realizing that (for some crazy reason) I left it inside. Oh, the panic I once felt when I was walking into a meeting and then realized that I left my phone in the car. I dashed back outside so quickly you'd think I had left a baby unattended on a hot summer's day. I knew everything I needed to cover in the meeting, but the thought of not being able to check the notes on my cell was just too uncomfortable. I literally couldn't bear it. I could no longer ignore the string of constant red flags popping up, like my recurring nightmares of losing my phone. In reality, the nightmare is what's actually happening when I *don't* "lose" my phone every now and then! I definitely had "nomophobia." Seriously, it's a thing; it stands for No Mobile Phone Phobia. Apparently, I'm not alone. These numbers from a January 2018 article by Arianna Huffington titled "The Great Awakening" are staggering:[40]

- There are 2.6 billion smartphone users worldwide—a number expected to climb to 6.1 billion by 2020.

- The top ten users of smartphones touch their phones an average of 5,427 times each day.

- The rest of us clock in at 2,617 touches per day.

- Between midnight and 5 A.M., 87 percent of participants in a study checked their phones at least once.

- Over 70 percent of Americans sleep next to or with their phone.

That's a heck of a lot of phone activity. This next fact may help reduce the amount of texting that you do. Have you heard of "text neck"? It's a spine ailment from, you guessed it, overuse of the cell phone.

> ## It's Science!
>
> Orthopedic spine specialist Dr. Kenneth Hansraj says, "The human head weighs about a dozen pounds. But as the neck bends forward and down, the weight on the cervical spine begins to increase. At a 15-degree angle, this weight is about 27 pounds, at 30 degrees it's 40 pounds, 60 degrees it's 60 pounds. That's the burden that comes with staring at a smartphone."[41] Researchers confirm that, over time, this can eventually lead to surgery. Orthopedic surgeons, 1; Chronic Texters, 0.

ARE PHONES MAKING US LOSE OUR MEMORY?

Another habit I wanted to change in regard to my phone came after hearing Dan Harris's "10% Happier" podcast with guest Manoush Zomorodi. Zomorodi mentioned that photography has changed the way we use our memory and I found this kind of scary. "When you take constant pictures, you're outsourcing your memory to your phone. By doing that, we may not actually remember ever having been in the moment. There's less than a second of a moment where we to decide to get out our phone or not. Ask yourself, Do I need this? Will it help me? Am I having a good experience that doesn't need to be captured? It's about being smarter with tech and choosing your moments in real life."[42]

That was a powerful example of how easily we can change our brain chemistry with technology and not even realize it. Taking ourselves *out* of a meaningful moment? That hit me hard; that's the opposite of what I always try to do. Self-awareness is a great place to start to sense the digital overexposure, stress, habitual behavior that may be innocently occurring in your life. Taking your "tech temperature" will help you begin to notice if you've got the fever.

TAKE YOUR TECH TEMPERATURE

If you haven't taken an official inventory of your time spent with eyes glued to your various screens or gotten a true idea of how many times per day you habitually reach for your smartphone, begin to notice these and other digital habits for the next twenty-four to forty-eight hours. Ask yourself these questions and then start to take notice. Hint: Write things down so you don't lose count!

- Do you have an automatic reflex that reaches for the phone the minute you finish a task or the minute your mind could be still and quiet for a nano second?

- Are you mindlessly skimming feeds for what you thought was 10 minutes but you're approaching an hour or even longer?

- Is your phone turned on and close to your bed when you go to sleep? Does this lead to checking email during your 3 A.M. trip to the bathroom?

- Are you feeling brain fog at the end of the day from not taking conscious digital breaks to recharge?

- Are you constantly distracted by app notifications?

- Are you paying full attention to people when you're with them, or are you multitasking with your phone?

- Are you becoming less productive but feel like you're always working?

- Do you do everything electronically and rarely have work or business conversations in person or via phone?

- Are you known for being a "fast responder"? We all have colleagues who we *know* will answer our text immediately. Is that you? (It was me!)

All yes answers are red flags. Again, like with the self-awareness testing in Chapter 1, be nonjudgmental. Look at this as research. Once you've seen your habits, think about what surprised you and exactly what you want to change. Draft some ideas about a possible new structure of your time that you can turn into a new routine or at least some sort of new boundaries. That's what it is: boundaries. Become more protective of your time. (More on this in Chapter 5.)

In an *Entrepreneur* article titled "All Business Is Personal: Employees Need Human Connections at Work," writer Harry West says, "Employee engagement starts with meaningful relationships. Companies that don't support those interactions will see productivity tank as their best talent walks. Engaging a workforce is a company-wide effort that must start at the top for any real change to occur. Digital initiatives already have revolutionized how companies interact with external stakeholders. They'd do well to apply the same techniques in their relationships with internal stakeholders."[43] Can you initiate something within your office for a collective time to unplug? It may seem counterproductive but it's not! Connecting with colleagues can lead to brainstorming, shifting perspectives, and the desire to collaborate.

CREATIVITY REQUIRES UNPLUGGING

You can't use up creativity.
The more you use, the more you have.
— MAYA ANGELOU

Creativity is a huge part of success. There's nothing like the feeling of creating something from nothing. Whether it's a business, a book, an article, a product, a service—in whatever form it materializes, it came from an idea while you were in a mindset that was conducive to creativity. If you're not making time for your brain to rest and your mind to be free, clear, and open for creativity, then you are limiting your success. Sounds harsh, but it's true. Plus, being creative feels fun and youthful, right? It takes me back to the days where a fresh pack of colored construction paper was like being handed 100 opportunities to create something new and exciting. (Or was that just me?) It made me giddy to think about how I'd fill each page. Think about each day as a piece of that construction paper, an opportunity to create something that's uniquely yours, and that will help you accomplish your goals. Yes, occasionally my artwork didn't appear as beautiful as I'd hoped, so I'd crumple up a page and toss it. That'll happen with creating your opportunities as well, but instead of calling them trash, think of them as lessons, mistakes, and failures that you *can* move on from to create something new. There's more paper, there's another day, another opportunity to get creative again. Breathe. Whatever that creative process looks like for you, it begins by making the mental space of creating a blank canvas.

It's Science!

In a *Forbes* article titled "Your Brain Unplugged," writer Lawton Ursrey says, "You know those moments of brilliance in the moments you least expect—when you're not focused on something in particular—middle of the night, in the shower, when you're relaxing outside. . . . That's the Default Mode Network or Resting State Network . . . Moments of idleness that produce creative ideas. Aha moments will occur when you disconnect because the Default Mode Network is processing reflective thoughts of yourself, spatial ideas, and visual information—when you're busy that activity is suppressed."[44]

When was the last time you had an amazing "aha" moment while at your laptop or phone? As science will tell you, probably very rarely. We need space and a wandering mind to get our creative juices flowing. Some need quiet; others need music. I get my most creative thoughts when I wake up in the middle of the night or when I'm on my yoga mat or taking a walk at the beach. Do you know where you need to be to get into your creative zone? If you don't know where that place is, find it and make at least one weekly date with yourself there to be unplugged and let your mind wander free, enjoying the scenery and opening your mind to nurturing creativity again. Schedule unplugged time to open your mind and be present. Deep breaths. Let your mind take a walk and see where it goes.

STUDIES ARE UNDERWAY FOR DIGITAL WELLNESS

The conversations are happening; researchers, scientists, journalists, and wellness advocates are all working on figuring out how tech is affecting our health. Help is on the way for us to be able to make informed decisions on the importance of managing our digital lives in business. The Global Wellness Institute is a nonprofit organization that educates people all over the globe on the benefits of preventive health and wellness. In April 2018, the Institute released a white paper titled "Wellness in the Age of the Smartphone" as part of its Digital Wellness Initiative. The initiative is led by Jeremy McCarthy (Group Director of Spa & Wellness, Mandarin Oriental Hotel Group). I spoke with Jeremy about his research and agree with his cautious perspective on tech in the paper: "The problem with technology is not that it is bad, it is that it is too good. The allure of technology and all its many benefits draws us away from other aspects of life. Our modern devices are so tantalizing, in fact, that we sometimes don't realize the sacrifices we are making along the way. While enjoying technology, we choose sedentary activities over movement, we choose virtual relationships over real ones, and we choose to consume information rather than reflect or take action on the things we have learned."[45]

The white paper analysis is eye-opening and the mission "is not to denounce technology, but to fully appreciate and recognize the benefits while creating greater awareness of the associated opportunity costs." Check out the paper if you want to read more. You also might consider your habits within the six areas where the "Wellness in the Age of the Smartphone" study found that technology negatively impacts our health: sleep; inactivity, obesity, and physiological health; mental wellness; social relationships and loneliness; distraction and safety; and productivity. Are any one of those sectors suffering a bit in your life?

In addition to the Global Wellness Institute, many advocates exist for living healthy, tech-centric business lives. One outspoken activist, author, and speaker for wellness in the business sector who clearly stands out is Arianna Huffington. She founded the Huffington

Post in 2005, sold it to AOL in 2011, and left in 2016 to launch a new digital wellness platform called Thrive Global. She's a prolific writer about the topic of well-being after breaking her cheekbone while falling asleep at her desk, overworked and exhausted. Huffington has been a leading voice in workplace wellness and the importance of a proper night's sleep ever since. Thrive Global is a wealth of health-centric inspiration, content, and resources that covers a great deal for workplace wellness in both corporate and small business sectors. She has formed impactful partnerships recently with brands like SAP and Zenefits to use technology and innovation to help us all move from "surviving to thriving" as we learn to create a healthy relationship with technology and innovation. In Huffington's February 2018 article titled "The Great Awakening," she described 2018 as the year of the "Great Reckoning": "The year in which we're forced to decide what we want from technology and what irreducible parts of our humanity we want to safeguard and protect. The stakes are huge. . . . We need to be in control of our technology."[46] Hear, hear!

Google recently launched a new initiative called Digital Wellbeing (*https://wellbeing.google*). It's not surprising that this occurs at Google (more on other mindful Googlers in Chapter 6). The new website describes the initiative as "Dedicated to building technology that is truly helpful for everyone. We're creating tools and features that help people better understand their tech usage, focus on what matters most, disconnect when needed, and create healthy habits for the whole family. We're committed to giving everyone the tools they need to develop their own sense of digital wellbeing. So that life, not the technology in it, stays front and center."[47] The initiative was announced at Google's annual developers conference and is aimed at people focusing on JOMO (Joy of Missing Out) rather FOMO (Fear of Missing Out).

Former Google program manager Tristan Harris has been a passionate and vocal activist since 2013 about how digital products were "not being designed with the consumers' best interests in mind" and that technology in fact is "hijacking our minds." His insights about technology needing a new set of morals led to a new role for him within Google: Design Ethicist. He left Google in 2016 to work full-time on building a nonprofit initiative called Time Well Spent; he also founded the Center for Humane Technology (*http://humanetech.com*) to work on "reversing the digital attention crisis and realigning tech with humanity's best interest."[48] He is a man on a mission. It'll be interesting to see how the other tech giants get involved in this movement. There will definitely be some friction as the business models of the biggest social media platforms are based on the attention economy, and we will all be learning to better manage our attention. Let's stay tuned on this.

BUSINESS OPPORTUNITIES IN DIGITAL WELLNESS

Unplugged is the new luxury. After years of total smart-phone devotion, I'm craving my pre-tech days. It's too bad that kids today will never know that feeling of being completely free from devices. Unplugging is my new luxury and breath is my antidote to tech. None of my online behavioral tweaks feels as liberating as stepping away from my screens for a few minutes, a couple of hours, or even a full day. That's progress. There's a sense of freedom and connection back to myself and others that I was sorely missing. I was craving that Savasana stillness and quiet to slow my mind down, to feel calm and grounded. It's empowering to take back control of your time, focus, creativity, alertness, and productivity by forming new strategies for your unplugged life. Refresh. Renew. Recharge. Breathe.

With every common problem come opportunities to provide effective solutions. I'm excited to see new products and services that help us on the journey to digital balance, workplace wellness, and better overall health and well-being. It may take the act of *paying* in order for us to disconnect sometimes. There are retreats for digital detox where you pay to "surrender" your phone for the weekend while focusing on mindfulness and healthy activity. What if hotels or restaurants charged us a premium to take possession of our phone when we arrive so that we could fully enjoy the experience? Would you be willing to pay? Another idea is having contraptions or special pockets right inside our purses or briefcases in which we can lock our phones—to be unlocked in a special way and only after a certain period of unplug. I experienced something similar recently at a concert where we were not allowed to use cell phones during the performance. When you entered the venue, security guards put your cell phone in a case that could only be unlocked by them. (This was not done for the sake of wellness, though; it was done to keep the show off the Internet.) If you needed to use your phone, you could walk over to an area in the lobby to have it unlocked to make your call or check your email. Yes, of course, I was initially uncomfortable with the situation. I also have to admit that I found myself unconsciously reaching for my phone even though I knew it was locked up. It was a powerful experience because after a few deep breaths, I was in the moment and the concert absolutely flew by. I'm sure I remember a lot more about it because I didn't outsource the memory to my phone.

Numerous apps, products, and wellness services are emerging in this space, but there's still lots of room for more products to improve our digital wellness and enhance brain health, energy, posture, and sleep. I'm experimenting right now with blue light-blocking glasses, which help block some of the blue light that comes from our screens. I'm trying to commit to use tech now only if it brings value in the moment. I've made a list of priorities and time frames, and I'm managing my digitally connected behavior with breath and a heightened sense of self-awareness. By the way, it takes anywhere from a couple of weeks to a couple of months for a rewiring trick to become a new habit, so be patient. Breathe. You can make the change. Sometimes it takes a village to help make these types of changes, so when you do decide that you're going to make changes, let your colleagues know. That way, you feel accountable to making the changes and they understand why you may no longer be responding to texts or emails within three minutes. Digital wellness can no longer be an afterthought; it's got to move front and center, top of mind.

IDEAS FOR UNPLUGGED TIME

Here are some simple yet impactful ideas for "unplugging":

- Go old school: Sit down with a cup of tea or coffee at a cafe and don't touch your phone; put it out of sight. Do you remember the pretech days at Starbucks? You may have had a book or newspaper with you, or you may have just enjoyed your beverage. Rest your brain.

Get comfortable with being confident enough to just sit and not be looking at a screen. We've come to feel odd if we're in public and just looking around. Breathe and relax. People watching is a lost art, and it's super entertaining.

- Buy some (real paper) books, magazines, or newspapers and keep them readily available and at your office. Enjoy the experience of unplugged reading where you won't be disturbed by notifications or Googling something while reading that leads you down a rabbit hole. That's my problem—clicking on links within articles that lead to more articles and links and ten minutes somehow become an hour.

- Redesign some of your lunch times to be unplugged. Don't eat in front of your screen. Schedule some lunches or business dinners around the idea of fully enjoying being unplugged and engaged.

- Get outside for even for ten minutes during the day. Go for a walk alone or with a colleague. Work doesn't always have to be done in the office. Take a business call or participate in a brainstorming session while walking outside. Nature is such a powerful rejuvenator. Fresh air is medicine for the soul. Sunshine is a vitamin. Breathe it in whenever possible!

- Find pleasure in being present in a good moment at work. See what happens to your mind and body when you heighten your senses by being present for a couple of minutes. The next time something great happens, soak it up. Breathe into it. Stop time to consciously enjoy and acknowledge an accomplishment.

- Turn off your phone for one hour a day. It's silly how empowering this can be.

- Think about what you used to do that made you feel creative and/or happy and completely in your element . . . that thing you did where minutes turned into hours while you enjoyed making, creating, tinkering, or doing. Go do that again . . . without your phone.

- Say goodnight to your electronics at least two hours (okay, maybe start with one) before bedtime, and don't even *think* of touching it if you wake up in the middle of the night.

According to Larry Rosen, professor of social psychology at California State University at Dominguez Hills and author of *iDisorder: Understanding Our Obsession with Technology and Overcoming Its Hold on Us*, "Exposure to the blue light from a device stops production of the sleep hormone melatonin, so it's harder to fall asleep."[49] Keep your phone out of your bedroom at night. Breathe through that temptation.

We need to unplug so that we can experience more conscious connectedness and not lose precious minutes, hours, days, weeks, months, or even years (it adds up!) of moments that we aren't fully experiencing. If the thought of having to reorganize your digital life has you clenching your jaw right now, relax. You'll figure it out. Baby steps. Start with 3DB and a positive intention to make little changes that will enhance your life. Remember, you're not taking something away but rather you're giving yourself something back in the form of time, connection, health, and ultimately more success.

5

TURN YOUR MORNING ROUTINE INTO A POWERFUL RITUAL

Morning Routine. You can make up your bed,
make up your face, but before you leave the
house, make up your mind.

—ANONYMOUS

As you consider changing some of your digital habits, the most impactful place to start is in the morning. If you currently wake up and automatically start scrolling email and social or news feeds, it's like eating sugary cereal for breakfast. You know better. It may feel good in the moment, but you regret it soon afterward, mentally and physically. Focusing on incoming things (that often incite negative emotions) can easily set you back first thing in the morning because you begin the day reacting instead of prioritizing and preparing. Morning routine is a key part of the day for highly successful people, and most routines include a workout of some sort as well as, you guessed it, mindfulness exercises. Time is our most precious commodity; that's why people are so curious about how uber successful business leaders spend their morning. You can find books, articles, and podcasts all about this topic. What can we learn from their morning rituals? One thing is that there's real momentum that comes from starting your day off right—owning your time.

IT'S SCIENCE!

Ron Friedman, author of *The Best Place to Work,* says via *Harvard Business Review,* "Typically, we have a window of about three hours where we're really, really focused. We're able to have some strong contributions in terms of planning, in terms of thinking, in terms of speaking well. And if we end up squandering those first three hours reacting to other people's priorities for us, which is ultimately what voice mail, or email is, a list of other people's requests for our time, that ends up using up our best hours and we're not quite as effective as we could be."[50]

What's *not* happening first thing for most highly successful professionals are things like email, texts, social feeds—things that cause distractions and make time disappear. If you've been in the weeds with emails, texts, and scrolling first thing and not then feeling energized when you head to work, you're going to be blown away by the difference that it makes to begin the day focused on your own goals first. Breathe. Get centered, strong, and grounded first, even for just a few minutes.

> *When you begin your day with mental clarity from slow, deep breathing, you take control of your priorities and put yourself first. You're less reactive and more proactive all day long. Taking a few deep breaths and choosing a positive intention for the day (Breathing Like a Boss) turns a routine morning into a powerful morning ritual with meaning and momentum.*

You don't have to have an indulgent spa–type of morning to make an impactful change. Even just a few minutes of breathing and connecting your mind and body is enough to connect with positive thoughts, energy, and confidence. Getting mindful about your intentions for your day are just as important as setting intentions for your business. It brings clarity and a strategic effort to all of your actions. Don't worry; you don't need to set an alarm and make extra time. If nothing else, just begin by making the first five or six minutes of your day all about setting you up with energy that's in sync with your goals. Fuel yourself with "super charged" oxygen—deep breaths that are powered with positive intention. Every day is yet another chance to get closer to your goals, to improve and evolve, to perform at new optimal levels, and to be the energy that others want to work with and work for. Remember, it's your choice how you think and feel. If you haven't been consciously choosing, you've been allowing outside forces to guide your day, week, month, or year. Morning is the best time to reinforce *your* choice and embed it in your mind and body. There's something very exciting about the clean slate of a new morning—a fresh start. If you're *Breathing Like a Boss* in the A.M., your day can take on the specific energy of whatever you want to manifest before you leave the house. You can let go of yesterday, not think too much about tomorrow, and focus on this new opportunity of *now*. Bring it on! There's no better time to be still, get quiet even for just a few minutes and make up your mind about how you're going to *be*. Decide according to your priorities and goals. As you begin to add breath practice into your life, make morning the first place for integration. You'll see the effects on Day One, especially if you set a reminder for 3DB, three times a day to build your new habit.

Successful people seem to have non-negotiable morning rituals so that they control their time until they are officially working and accessible. Until then, they don't give others the opportunity to disrupt their energy, priorities, or creativity. They're extremely protective of their morning time and will defend it vigorously. Arriving at work in a bad state of mind can ruin the whole day. Steffanie Wilk, associate professor of management and human resources at The Ohio State University's Fisher College of Business, says, "We saw that employees could get into these negative spirals where they started the day in a bad mood and just got worse over the course of the day. Starting off at work wearing rose-colored glasses—or gray glasses—shapes the way we perceive events the rest of the day."[51] *Breathe Like a Boss* in the morning so that you don't ever leave the house with gray glasses.

One of the easiest ways to add breath into your morning as you initially begin this new practice is to attach your deep breaths to some simple, feel-good, stretching movements. These stretches ease your mind and body into the morning in the gentlest way. Again, these exercises don't take more than a few minutes but will get your energy going in the right direction. Here are my five favorite yoga-inspired stretches to ease into your morning and activate your breath:

Arm Raises: You can do these while still sitting in bed or standing up if you prefer. On an inhale, raise your arms above your head, touching your hands together, and on the exhale, lower your arms. Inhaling and exhaling while raising and lowering your arms. Simple, but it get the juices flowing for feeling in sync and connected.

Side Stretch: Again, either while still sitting in bed or standing. On an inhale, raise your arms above your head, clasp them together, and side bend to the left on an inhale; then come back to center on the exhale. Inhale and side bend to the right; exhale back to center. Repeat a few times with long, deep breaths.

Forward Folds: Sitting or standing. Raise your arms above your head on the inhale; on the exhale, do an easy rounded forward fold. Stay forward for a few deep breaths and then move in and out of it a few times with each inhale and exhale. Forward folding brings on relaxation, especially when you're not focused on the actual stretching; simply fold and relax.

Cow/Cat Pose: This simple flow stimulates the kidneys and adrenal glands. Start on your hands and knees with your wrists under your shoulders, and your knees under your hips. Center your head and gaze downward.

1. Moving into Cow Pose: Inhale as you gently arch your back. Lift your chin and chest, and gaze up toward the ceiling. Move your shoulders away from your ears.

2. Moving into Cat Pose: As you exhale, draw your belly to your spine and round your back toward the ceiling. The crown of your head moves toward the floor, and your chin gently moves toward your chest.

Repeat by inhaling back into Cow Pose, and then exhale as you return to Cat Pose. It's a great way to warm up your spine and get some deep breaths flowing. Feel free to make it your own and maybe add some circular movement to continue to slowly wake up the spine and stretch your toes out while you're moving too. Waking up the toes and bottoms of the feet is very energizing.

Heart Openers/Upper Back Bends: I love doing heart openers in the morning—they (figuratively) open the chest and heart and are very energizing. Stand tall, shoulders up and back, clasp your hands behind your back, and arch your upper back just a bit while inhaling and exhaling. Be mindful to not overarch your low back; tuck your tailbone slightly under to help protect the low back. You can also raise and lower your clasped hands a few times while inhaling and exhaling. 3DB is so empowering as you open your heart to the day. If you're comfortable leaning your head back, you can do that; otherwise, you still get a heart-opening/upper back bend with your head looking straight ahead.

Attaching the breath to these stretches is an easy way to begin to breathe in the morning. These stretches paired with slow deep breaths wake up your mind, body, and positive energy. One of my yoga teachers always used to say, "We are only as young as our spine is supple." So, I like to breathe into moving my spine around a bit in the morning. It gets everything flowing and I've meditated without even realizing it. These stretches also help to build self-awareness about your posture. As you begin to breathe full, deep breaths, you'll notice that your posture improves. You stand taller, your shoulders are adjusted up and back, your tailbone is tilted under, and you're always at the ready to fill your belly and expand the space that you're in. It feels good to expand your mind, your mood, and your posture. Speaking of posture, I heard (professor and researcher at Harvard Business School) Amy Cuddy speak at an event and was inspired by her "Power Pose" philosophy. If you want to take some deep breaths while standing in the "victorious" position to start your day, that'll also immediately improve your energy. Cuddy's TED talk, "Your Body May Shape Who You Are," has been viewed 47 million times. Her research on power posing and "how your body position influences others and even your own brain" is fascinating.[52]

Power poses paired with deep breaths can be a great morning ritual. Stand tall, feet a little wider than hip distance and arms stretched out overhead in a "V" (victorious) position. Think of the position that athletes automatically do when they've won a competition. I like to stretch out my fingers as well and breathe in the energy of the pose. It literally makes you feel ready for victories—all day long.

One other thing you might want to add to your morning stretch and breath session is—drumroll please—aromatherapy. It's *that* good. It's not just for spa visits; it's scientifically proven to affect our emotions and so requires a proper mention for those who are not taking advantage of this added "multiplier" of breath. I've been a fan of aromatherapy sprays and oils ever since exhibiting at the spa trade shows back in the early 1990s. Using your sense of smell helps to release serotonin and dopamine (the "good mood" neurotransmitters). Smell is highly emotive.

Aromatherapy spray or essential oils add that extra something special in the mornings to start the day; it's nature's gift for your sense of smell and your brain. Keep some aromatherapy spray/oil by your bedside and breathe in the scent of orange or jasmine or fennel first thing. There are many uplifting fragrances to choose from, so find a scent that makes you smile. Scents are also attached to memories; you'll want to pick a fragrance that is attached to a positive memory. For example, maybe a certain floral scent reminds you of your honeymoon. I use aromatherapy sprays and essential oils throughout the day, keeping some in my handbag, my car, and my desk, and the house is always stocked up for a quick aromatherapy boost. There's always a new fragrance to enjoy. Adding in a scent from nature to your breathing ritual takes it to another level. It's experiential.

It's Science!

According to NIH Research Study: "The sense of smell plays an important role in the physiological effects of mood, stress, and working capacity. Electrophysiological studies have revealed that various fragrances affected spontaneous brain activities and cognitive functions, which are measured by an electroencephalograph (EEG). In the last few decades, many scientific studies were conducted to investigate the effect of inhalation of aroma on human brain functions. Studies have suggested a significant role for olfactory stimulation in the alteration of cognition, mood, and social behavior."[53]

I'm a big fan of brands that are completely natural, with no synthetic toxins or chemicals so you can inhale abundantly. Aromatherapy is a natural tool to boost your mood and energy. Give this simple pleasure a try as you deepen your breath practice. Once you begin to use aromatherapy, you'll enjoy the way it can stimulate your mind, encourage positive emotions, and even boost your creativity.

Since Mother Nature is the absolute best aromatherapy, whenever possible simply breathe in the natural energy of the ocean, mountains, green grass, rain, flowers, and herbs. Breathe in the expansive energy of the full moon, or the horizon, the warmth of the sunshine, the clarity of a bright, crystal clear sky. When you're outside anywhere, stop and "smell the roses"; take 3DB and let nature energize and inspire you. Breathing in the great outdoors is another simple yet powerful tool for mood, energy, and therefore success.

> *"I only went out for a walk, and finally concluded to stay out till sundown, for going out, I found, was really going in."*
> —JOHN MUIR

Everyone enjoys different aromatherapy scents, but if you need a starting point (to bring the beauty of nature inside), here are a few of my favorite uplifting scents, especially for morning: citrus, such as orange, bergamot, neroli, grapefruit, yuzu, mandarin, and lime; florals such as jasmine, ylang-ylang, and geranium; and plants/herbs, such as fennel, rosemary, mint, lavender, and white sage. The combinations of empowering and uplifting scents are endless. The power of scent will likely surprise you if you haven't been utilizing it. It not only activates awareness for deep breathing but also initiates positive energy. When you get your mind–body connection in sync first thing, it sets you up with a solid foundation for moving into the nitty-gritty of your day. No more waking up and not knowing what's going to make you feel strong, focused, and grounded. We all have different ideas about what makes a productive morning, so make your ritual unique to you, but make it something special that you look forward to. You deserve an upgraded morning ritual. Autopilot morning is like shallow breath; it may get the job done but nothing special comes from it. And when you've made the effort to take control of your morning and given yourself what makes you feel your energetic best, you're invested in carrying that energy through the day. If that feeling fades, now you know how easy it is to regroup or refocus with a lion's breath or 3DB. Breathe. Be present. Be positive. Good morning!

> ## IT'S SCIENCE!
>
> "The olfactory sense has a unique intimacy with emotion. Unlike other senses, olfactory neuroanatomy is intertwined, via extensive reciprocal axonal connections, with primary emotion areas including the amygdala, hippocampus, and orbitofrontal cortex. . . . Odors can be used as contextual cues to cognitions, behavior, and mood." Taken from an NIH Study by Andrew J. Johnson.[54]

DO CHALLENGING THINGS IN THE MORNING

Breathing Like a Boss in the morning kicks up your energy, making it a good time to tackle difficult tasks. You feel stronger mentally because you're present and in the moment. Researchers have said that we are the most productive a couple hours after waking up and for a few hours after that. So strike while the iron is hot in the A.M. Do the most difficult tasks first and cross them off your list. This approach will add to your momentum as well; you won't carry around the dread of having to deal with something difficult later. Procrastination is definitely not a trait of those uber successful business leaders. Also, when you go through your day with the weight of looming tasks you allow that low-level chronic stress to continue to simmer. Author and entrepreneur James Clear says, "Success usually comes down to choosing the pain of discipline over the ease of distraction."[55]

IN GOOD TIME AND WITH GOOD TIMING

In my pre-yoga days, I was an impatient and impulsive entrepreneur. I wanted instant results and when they didn't happen (because good things take time), I'd get frustrated and disappointed. After finding my breath, I also found an entirely new perspective on both time and timing.

> **Time:** *How we spend and experience our hours, days, weeks, months, and years.* The more you experience mindful breathing, the more you can slow down your internal pace. Time changes a bit. Accepting this has been an incredible benefit for me. Yes, the years still fly by, but the hours and days feel more manageable. You'll find yourself less rushed and more strategic and productive. When you set yourself up well in the morning, you begin to work from a different pace that allows you to fit more into your day. Once you begin to manage your distractions (whether tech related or just the way your mind works), you're no

longer a slave to the clock. You become much more in tune with time. I usually know what time it is within a three-minute span, even when I wake up in the middle of the night. It's an odd game that came to be years ago. My internal clock is now lit! Breath also slowed my pace so that I could "work in the zone" more often. But more recently (post–tech revolution), it became difficult again to stay focused. I found myself falling back into my old tendencies of shorter attention span. Breath continues to save me when it comes to focus. It may ebb and flow, but you'll know how to breathe your way back into focusing for larger chunks of time. If you can change your mood and mindset in just one minute with a few deep breaths, imagine what you can accomplish if you get focused on one task for three or four hours, in the zone?

Don't say you don't have enough time.
You have exactly the same number of hours
per day that were given to Helen Keller,
Pasteur, Michelangelo, Mother Teresa,
Leonardo da Vinci, Thomas Jefferson, and
Albert Einstein.
— H. JACKSON BROWN, JR.

Timing: This is all about being in the right the place at the right time, being open to opportunities, and being patient. Breath has also given me a deep appreciation for understanding the importance of timing and being able to wait things out. The first big purchase order that I mentioned in Chapter 1 exemplifies one of my first lessons with timing and patience. Breath has also opened my mind to the fact that I do believe in good timing; waiting for all of the stars to all align rather than just expecting something to happen just because I think I'm ready. Usually while waiting for things to happen, I end up doing more work and getting more prepared, so it's a good thing.

THE SCIENCE OF GOOD TIMING

I recently learned an interesting nuance on time and timing from Daniel Pink, author of *When: The Scientific Secrets of Perfect Timing*. It was on one of my favorite podcasts: "10% Happier with Dan Harris." Pink talks about his research on how we should consider doing certain tasks at specific times during the day to achieve the best results. He says, "Timing is not an art, it's a science." I can clearly see where breath can come into play as well since not everything can be coordinated to the scientific timeline. In the podcast, Daniel Pink explains the science of timing:

OUR DAY IS DIVIDED INTO THREE STAGES

Pink says that our day is divided into three stages: 1. Peak, 2. Trough, and 3. Recovery. These stages ring true for both mood and performance. His research shows that student standardized test scores drop considerably when tests are taken in the afternoon compared to morning. Pink adds that "Our cognitive abilities don't remain the same throughout the day. They change in a predictable way and they change in ways that are more extreme way than we realize." Here are Pink's recommendations for working in conjunction with the timing of your brainpower:

Peak/Morning Phase: Do analytic work that requires focus, attention, and vigilance.

Trough/Early-Mid Afternoon Phase: When you're in your "trough," apparently you aren't even close to performing at your peak. Pink suggests this is the time of day for administrative tasks like emails. He explains that doing difficult analytic work during your trough phase is "like bicycling into ferocious headwinds." *This* is where self-awareness and breath can come in handy as an extra source of power.

Recovery/Late Afternoon, Evening Phase: By late afternoon your mood has come back up naturally, but Pink says, "We are less vigilant; so it's a great time for brainstorming or iterative kinds of work."

Pink adds, "Changing the time of day that you do something can vary your performance level by 20%. Usually we're unintentional about when we do something, especially in meeting planning. Organizations are completely blind about it. Scheduling a meeting is a strategic decision." We can be conscious of this timing in business applications, but it's not always going to unfold accordingly. Sometimes you *have* to give a speech at 3 P.M. or do a pitch presentation at 2 P.M. during what would be your trough. But don't worry—you've got your breath, intention, and visualization to help give you back that 20 percent variance for doing a task at a "non-optimal" time![56]

TIMING IS TOP FACTOR FOR SUCCESS IN START-UPS

Bill Gross, founder of Idea Lab, studied over 200 companies to find out what makes startups succeed and fail. He talked about his findings in his TED talk (viewed over 5 million times), admitting surprise when learning that timing was the biggest factor in making the difference between success and failure. Here are his top five factors for success:

- Timing, 42%
- Team/Execution, 32%
- Idea, 28%
- Business Model, 24%
- Funding, 14%

Gross says that the idea for a business isn't nearly as important as the timing. This is an interesting aspect to think about before you bring something to market.

Gross uses the example of Airbnb, and how many big investors passed on the idea because it seemed weird to rent your your home to strangers, but the timing made it simply brilliant. He says, "It came out during the height of the recession when people needed extra money and that helped to overcome the objection of renting out their home to a stranger. Same thing with Uber, perfect timing as drivers were looking for extra money."[57]

Who would have thought that timing matters more than the idea, business model, funding, or the team? Be mindful of the needs of consumers and the marketplace; when your finger is on the pulse of what's missing, and you have a solution to a common problem for the masses, you're in the right place at the right time for success. This is where patience is a virtue. Sometimes holding onto an idea until the timing is right can be difficult but extremely important to keep in mind.

Necessity may be the mother of invention, but timing is everything!

CHEERS! UPGRADE YOUR MORNING BEVERAGE AND FUEL YOUR BRAIN

Okay, stay with me on this idea. One big benefit of *Breathing Like A Boss* and turning your morning routine into a powerful ritual is that you begin to make other upgrades because you've become self-aware of your body and you want to keep your energy at its best levels for success as often as possible. This is a holistic approach to your mind–body connection and the reason why I'm going to talk about your morning beverage. I've never met someone who doesn't have some sort of love affair with their morning beverage, but you might be lovin' the wrong drink for your best morning energy. It may just be a long-time habit that you don't even realize is causing a setback first thing in the morning. If you're serious about wanting to take charge of your energy in the morning, consider what you put into your body. It's science. Drinks can make or break your energy and focus. Swap the soda or whipped-cream-topped, sugar-filled shake for something more nourishing and satiating. Today, there are so many innovative ways to pack a punch in your morning coffee (or beverage) that I'm compelled to share my thoughts on some small but powerful ingredient ideas for your morning drink(s). What if your morning beverage (while still delicious) gave you the caffeine you love along with other superfoods or plant-based adaptogens that help increase your cognitive function? Yes, that's what I'm talking about: fueling your brain! Now, you see why I'm going here; it's part of the plan for setting your mind and body up with the right energy for success. I've become a bit (okay, *quite* a bit) obsessed with beverages over the past several years, because like breath, a nourishing morning beverage can set the tone for the day. It can also have longer-term health benefits when you make it part of your daily morning routine. Fall in love with morning drinks that up the ante cognitively and energetically. The options for customizing drinks (like breath) are endless, and you can make these at home (which saves time and money). Think turmeric almond milk latte, for example. Or mushroom-based coffee with adaptogens like lion's mane and chaga. I know, it sounds "so L.A.," but it's coming to a health food store or cafe near you soon too. Adaptogens are natural ingredients that help your body adapt to stressors. These plants, herbs, and leaves have been around for thousands of years and (like meditation) are finally becoming mainstream. Think of adaptogens as fuel for your brain and energy without having to do anything besides sip and breathe. If you're going to be drinking anyway, why not make it a more functional (and delicious) drink? Ingredients like superfoods, adaptogens, herbs, greens, proteins, bone broths, healthy fats, and collagen have rocked my beverage world and have become readily available in health food stores and cafes beyond just L.A. and New York. I really look forward to my morning lineup of beverages because they're functional, healthy, and delicious and they make me feel energized and clear on a new level. If I'm working from home, I make drinks all day long not only because I enjoy them, but because it's a chance to breathe and savor each nourishing experience while continuing to fuel my brain and body. When it comes to food and drinks that improve our cognitive function, I've been inspired by Dr. Lisa Mosconi, neuroscientist, nutritional counselor and author of *Brain Food*.

IT'S SCIENCE!

In an article titled "A Scientist's Guide to Eating for Brain Health," Dr. Mosconi says, "Our diet affects our minds and shapes the way we think, feel, and age. . . . Of all the organs in our bodies, the brain is the most easily damaged by a poor diet. The nutrients we get from the foods we eat are taken up into the bloodstream and carried into our brains. Once there, they replenish depleted storage, activate cellular reactions, and become the very fabric of our brains."[58]

That's important to grasp; our brain is the most easily damaged organ by poor food/drink choices. What you eat and drink in the morning immediately affects your brain as you begin your day. Beverages and breath are an empowering pairing. You'll quickly begin to notice the difference in your energy and clarity when you upgrade your drinks. Choosing drinks that nourish your mind and body leads to better choices and decisions all day long. Since beverages are a big part of my morning ritual, I feel compelled to share my favorite nourishing beverages that I hope will inspire you to whip up a few new drinks for an extra daily dose of energy and focus. There are so many incredible brain-boosting drink options. I'll list some ingredients so you can begin to experiment, but I will limit the recipes to my four go-to favorite morning ritual beverages. By the way, I will be doing more "Beverages & Breath" workshops and content online because these small changes make a big difference in clarity, productivity, creativity, mood, and focus.

Cleansing "Liquid Sunshine" Tonic: *This is a must for me every day first thing.*

Ingredients:

12 oz. hot water

Freshly squeezed lemon (half to a full lemon, depending on how tart you want your drink)

Splash of apple cider vinegar (Although it's an acquired taste, it helps your inner ecosystem and digestion; gut health is key for immunity.)

Ginger root, about 2–4 inches (I love the taste of ginger, but you can start with a smaller piece because ginger can get spicy.)

Turmeric root, ½–1 inch (It's a bright orange root and is the spice that gives curry its yellow color. It stains, so watch while cutting the root or drinking.)

You can use a small grater to grate the roots if you don't have a juicer machine. If you grate the ginger and turmeric root, put it into a small fine mesh strainer and then pour your hot water over it. Add in your lemon and apple cider vinegar. If you have a juicer, place the ginger and turmeric roots in, and then pour the juiced ginger/turmeric liquid into your hot water, and add lemon and apple cider vinegar. You'll have a beautiful, bright yellow drink. Ginger and turmeric are excellent for their anti-inflammatory and antioxidant properties. The drink is refreshing and detoxifying and gets your digestion moving. It wakes up your mouth, too, which is energizing. If you want to start this ritual using just hot water and lemon, there's still a lot of value in that. WellnessWithin.org explains the benefits of lemons:

- Lemons are full of vitamin C and contain saponins, which have antimicrobial properties.

- Lemons are high in potassium, which helps to control blood pressure, and it stimulates brain and nerve function.

- Lemons encourage the liver to produce quality bile, which is required for digestion. Vitamin C in fresh lemon juice helps the liver to produce the compound called glutathione, which aids in cleansing and regenerating the liver.

- The vitamins and minerals contained in lemons help to loosen toxins from the body, thereby flushing unwanted materials from the digestive tract. The citric acid in lemons helps maximize enzyme function, which stimulates and aids the liver in detoxification.

- Lemons are one of the most alkalizing foods for the body. Regular consumption of lemon water can help to remove overall acidity in the body, including uric acid in the joints, which is one of the primary causes of pain and inflammation.[59]

I usually make a double batch and drink it hot or cold throughout the day.

When life gives you lemons, make some liquid sunshine in the A.M.!

Energizing Green Juice: *Switch from processed orange to homemade green and start your day without the sugar spike. I've been green juicing for well over ten years. I love the pure energy I feel from the phytonutrients: vitamins, minerals, chlorophyll, and antioxidants. Green juice is made by extracting the fiber from greens or vegetables in a juicer machine. Since I'm sensitive to blood sugar spikes, I only juice with greens and little bit of lemon or ginger. I don't use other fruits like apple or pineapple. Reminder: This is a juice recipe, not a smoothie, so it goes through a juicer machine rather than a blender.*

Ingredients:

6–8 large stalks of celery

4–6 pieces of flat kale (Start small with the kale; this is what makes it very green tasting.)

1 lemon, peeled

1 large cucumber

2–3 inches of ginger root (optional)

Put all ingredients through the juicer, strain through a fine-mesh strainer if you like it completely clear, and enjoy! Think green lemonade. It's super hydrating, tart, cleansing, and energizing. This recipe makes approximately 16 ounces; it varies depending on the size of the celery and cucumber. When I make a big batch, I usually have half in the morning and save half for the afternoon in a tightly sealed glass jar in the refrigerator. If the result is too "green" for you, omit the kale or add half an apple or a little more lemon or ginger. Or you may surprise yourself and get used to enjoying the green, lemony taste. You can also use either celery or cucumber on its own as a green juice and experiment, adding one new green, fruit, veg, or citrus at a time. You're the chef; make whatever you enjoy!

Superfood Smoothies: *Smoothies are all the rage, but frequently they're made like frappuccinos, with way too much sugar. To clarify, smoothies are made in the blender, not a juicer. Occasionally, I'll crave a cold smoothie in the summer months and these have the added fiber of the greens, something you don't get from juicing. I usually prefer to eat something rather than drink a meal but these smoothies are filling and satisfying. When I'm in the mood for a smoothie, currently this is my go-to recipe:*

Ingredients:

2 big handfuls fresh organic spinach

1 handful frozen organic blueberries

1 teaspoon almond butter (any seed or nut butter; cashew, peanut, sunflower)

1 teaspoon chia seeds

1 cup almond milk (or other non-dairy milk alternative; cashew, hemp seed, or coconut milk)

Other optional add-ins:

Protein powder

Collagen Peptides (I enjoy the Vital Proteins brand)

Frozen steamed cauliflower florets (which have no flavor, I promise!)

Frozen uncooked zucchini slices

Frozen cooked sweet potato wedges

Yogurt; I love cashew- or coconut-based yogurts for nondairy options.

These smoothies are so versatile, you can add in whatever superfoods you love along with your veggies. You can blend it to be super smooth and drink it. Or you can keep it more on the thick side—for a smoothie bowl—and top it with all sorts of nuts, seeds, and superfood toppings like goji berries, hemp seeds, or flaxseeds.

In stores or cafes, banana is usually the main ingredient along with other high-sugar fruits like pineapple.

Making your smoothies at home controls the amount of sugar and also makes it much more affordable. Blueberries are the top pick in regard to fruits, according to Max Lugavere, author of Genius Foods: *"Of all commonly consumed fruits and vegetables, blueberries are among the highest in antioxidant capacity because of their abundance of compounds called flavonoids."[60]*

Espresso, Coffee, or Matcha Green Tea Latte:
I love a latte! These lattes are indulgent, empowering, and satiating. I cut out dairy many years ago, so I make my own almond milk. It may sound crazy, but once you make it, you can't go back to store bought—and it's so simple. (The recipe follows.) I'm a big fan of the new mushroom-based coffee from Four Sigmatic. It's chock-full of superfood mushrooms and a variety of adaptogens, and it doesn't taste like you think it might. In addition to coffee, they have other mushroom-based elixirs (cordyceps, lion's mane, and reishi are my favorites) that enhance your memory and brain function. I also love matcha green tea on its own or as a latte. Matcha comes only in powder form. It's full of antioxidants and has less caffeine than coffee. I add almond milk to most of my hot drinks and throw it in the blender to froth it up. I look forward to my delicious, creamy adaptogenic lattes every single

day and savor them with some deep breaths. Then on to business as usual. My mind and body are nourished, energized, and ready to be creative and productive. In the warmer months, these are also delicious cold, blended with ice.

"That's So L.A. Latte!" Recipe:

Make your hot water and add your espresso, coffee, tea, or matcha powder; then throw it in the blender with some warmed-up nut milk or milk of your choice. You can add in adaptogens or superfoods like chaga, cordyceps, collagen peptides, or even bone broth. Many people also enjoy adding in a fat like grass-fed butter or coconut oil. Experiment a bit to see what makes you feel energized, focused, and satiated.

Homemade Almond Milk: *I promise this doesn't take more than five minutes after you've soaked raw almonds overnight. If you're dairy free, nut milks are the best. You can cut this recipe in half to start. I make this full batch because I use it daily and it'll last up to five days.*

Ingredients:

2 cups raw almonds

6 cups filtered water (or you can use some or all coconut water)

Optional: Add a splash of vanilla extract or some vanilla bean.

Reusable fine mesh nut milk bag for straining

Soak raw almonds in water for 6–8 hours or overnight in the refrigerator. Drain the water out after soaking. Put the soaked almonds and 6 cups of water in a high speed blender and whirl it up for about 30 seconds.

Then, have a big bowl ready and pour the liquid through the fine-mesh reusable nut milk bag. Squeeze the bag until you've extracted all the liquid. You'll have a lot of almond milk and you'll also have the by-product that's left in the mesh bag, called almond pulp. Keep it refrigerated too. It can be used in baked goods or the simplest homemade crackers made from just the pulp and spices baked to crispy perfection. My husband looks forward to making these crackers weekly! One other option is as a sort of yogurt replacement; top it with berries, seeds, or nut butter, and enjoy. The great thing about creating beverages is that measurements are not critical (except with adaptogens). You can mix and match to your own taste preferences. The key is preparation: having these ingredients (and a blender and juicer) at home and ready to go. Here are some superfood/ adaptogenic ingredients to experiment with in your morning beverages or smoothies: bone broth, coconut water, cayenne, collagen peptides, raw cacao, acai, spirulina, maca, ginger, turmeric (and black pepper makes it more effective), chlorella, aloe, chia seeds, flaxseeds, hemp seeds, probiotics, goji berries, chaga, cordyceps, reishi, and lion's mane. Like breath, there are so many options. Enjoy the process of finding your favorite recipes.

Okay, back to the broader idea of the morning ritual. As you begin to breathe mindfully and strategically in the morning, start to treasure and protect your time, and fuel your brain with more functional drinks, it'll get easier to continue to have a handle on time and energy for the rest of the day. Morning routines evolve over time, so although you may have a routine now, it might be time to upgrade it. Take a minute to think about your morning routine. Visualize your mornings and ask yourself:

- Is there something that continually bothers you about your mornings? (running late, never have time to work out)

- What's one thing you'd like to remove from your mornings?

- What's one thing you want to start doing?

- How do you want to feel as you head into work?

Just as with figuring out how to best balance our digital lives, when mornings are more structured you can get some time back to spend on yourself. With simple breath techniques or even just easy, slow, deep breaths, you can make your morning feel indulgent with feel-good stretches, aromatherapy, positive thoughts and intentions, healthy/functional drinks, and dedicated time for you to be present, grounded, and strong for the day. Your morning ritual will evolve and require tweaking occasionally as your work–home life situations change. You can always iterate. Knowing when you need to make a change so that you fully own your time and energy is half the battle. Self-awareness once again; put your own oxygen mask on first, then you're fully able to help others all day long when you strategically make yourself accessible. Starting strong and knowing that your breath is at the ready all day, you're set up for success . . . and that's a powerful ritual!

6

C.E.'OMS: VISIONARIES OF MINDFUL BUSINESS

Great leaders have three things; inner light,
inner vision and inner strength.

—AMIT RAY

Incredible visionaries are leading the way for mindfulness in business. I call them *C.E.'Oms* and coined the term to represent a leader who takes charge with mindfulness. (Chief. Executive. Om. Representing yoga-inspired mindfulness/consciousness/well-being, a universal vibration.) Their stories are inspirational because they each show the impact that just one person can make when he or she decide to share his or her passion for mindfulness with authenticity and a contagious enthusiasm. I deeply admire the voice that these leaders give to spotlight the benefits of mindfulness and wellness in the business sector—not as an add-on but fully integrating it as the ethos of business. Infusing humanity back into our highly tech-driven business sector is no easy feat, and many of these C.E.'Oms started as a party of one and have simply shared their own experiences in a way that resonated with enough people to get funding and support from large organizations. It's exciting that corporate brands are much more open to the benefits of breath, mindfulness, and meditation in business because there are data to support the investment now.

Each of us can be a C.E.'Om wherever we work. Some of the C.E.'Oms featured in this chapter made such a difference within their large organization that either they felt compelled to leave their current position and take on a full-time mindfulness role or they left to take their "show on the road," and continue to be a voice for workplace wellness by launching their own consulting business or nonprofit to continue the mission. They've all been making massive progress. By sharing these C.E.'Om stories, I'm hoping other entrepreneurs, CEOs, executives, and employees will speak up where they lead or work and bring mindfulness to their colleagues, organizations, and teams. The time is now. Our minds are moving way too fast. Our internal speed cannot continue at the speed of digital. People are craving breath, meditation, stillness, mindfulness, well-being, and connection. Companies that offer wellness benefits and in-office perks will be the ones that attract and keep the best talent.

> *It's often the passionate grassroots party of one*
> *"bottom to top" efforts that make these initia-*
> *tives come to fruition. You can make a differ-*
> *ence. You can start a shift wherever you work.*
> *Mindfulness has proven to make people and*
> *businesses more effective, productive, engaging,*
> *healthy, and compassionate, and it also has pos-*
> *itive effects on the bottom line. That's win/win.*

Being aware of the collective energy at work is power-ful. These visionaries are leading the way for better business practices and more meaningful work from a place of positivity and benevolence—the collective greater good. Hopefully we'll see more full-time positions of Chief Mindfulness Officer and the like as we move into a new way of doing business that neutralizes the technology factor and emphasizes the humanity factor. I'll continue to share C.E.'Om stories online. In the meantime, here are just a few featured stories that inspire me.

C.E.'OM: YVON CHOUINARD, FOUNDER OF PATAGONIA

One of the most inspiring and longest-lasting examples of mindful intention, company culture, and leadership that I know of is the from the founder of Patagonia, Yvon Chouinard. He's been a C.E.'Om for over forty-five years. He's a self-proclaimed "reluctant business-man" who does everything with mindfulness to support what he truly values: high-quality products, environmental sustainability, and outdoor living. He has said that he and his original mountain-climbing business cohorts were "rebels from the consumer culture." He is definitely an inspiring case study in the "following your gut" school of business. Patagonia will continue to operate with those same core values well into the future as it is still a privately held, family-owned company and, as mentioned earlier, the B corp certification will keep those intentions intact for many years to come. Chouinard, now 79 years old, wrote a poignant book in 2005 titled *Let My People Go Surfing* about his company culture. The title gives you an idea of one of his core values and intentions. Patagonia headquarters is in Ventura, California, a beautiful beach town perfect for mixing business with pleasure. His passion for outdoor adventure, sustainability, and quality and his unique leadership style make Patagonia what it is today: a beloved billion-dollar global consumer brand. Here are highlights from his book and also from his C.E.'Om story in a terrific podcast segment from NPR, "How I Built This," with Guy Raz.[61]

CORE VALUES LEAD THE WAY

At his core, Chouinard is a a surfer, a craftsman, and an avid mountain climber, and says that growing up he played every sport. His entrepreneurial life began like many entrepreneurs—out of necessity. He and his mountain-climbing buddies needed a higher-quality piece of climbing hardware, so he taught himself how to be a blacksmith and made metal, reusable climbing pieces. These were to be the upgraded version of the single-use ones from Europe that were not the best quality. Even though their hardware cost ten times more than the European ones, Chouinard's product owned 80 percent of the market. Consumers agreed with Chouinard's priorities: producing top-quality products that also served the environment. The success from the initial climbing product led to expanding into clothing for the same customer base. A rugby shirt and climbing shorts were the first products that evolved into building a clothing company.

Realizing that he was in fact becoming a businessman without a college degree or any experience in clothing or business, Chouinard began to study business by reading books on Japanese management style and Scandanavian businesses. He wanted to find a better way to do business than what he saw in the United States. He says that he never "respected the profession." He wanted to do business in a way that felt good, that respected people as well as the planet. He says, "One of my favorite quotes is 'If you want to understand entrepreneurs, study juvenile delinquents.' They get creative and break rules, doing things their own way. They figure out something that nobody has thought about and do things differently. I love breaking the rules, that's the fun part of business." He and his wife were ahead of their time with a family-friendly office in the 1970s, offering maternity and paternity leave, flexible work schedules, and a childcare center at the office, where employees all interacted with the kids. Their company culture was authentically built around Chouinard's priorities of enjoying life while earning a living and doing business in unconventional ways for the greater good. As the years went by, Chouinard only held tighter to his intentions of being socially and environmentally responsible.

THE MORE YOU KNOW, THE LESS YOU NEED

Chouinard told Raz during his NPR podcast that his guiding philosophy has been as a student of Zen Buddhism most of his life. He's a believer in what he says is "the more you know, the less you need" philosophy. He's used this principle in his own life on many levels, including his ideas on clothing. He doesn't have a closet full of shiny new Patagonia outfits. That wouldn't feel right. He's content wearing clothes that are several years old because they're still useful. He feels a deep sense of responsibility to use Patagonia as a resource to share the philosophy of quality over quantity. Patagonia offers lifetime guarantees on its clothing. As Raz says, "Unlike most founders of a consumer product, Chouinard requests that people really think about things before they buy them and they don't advertise much at all." He was not driven by money, like most of his entrepreneurial peers. Patagonia now has the largest garment repair center in North America; it'll repair every piece of Patagonia clothing indefinitely. Patagonia also repairs any piece of clothing, whether Patagonia or not, from their mobile garment repair center that travels around. Patagonia became focused on more environment-friendly materials in the early 1990s, and mindful sourcing of fabrics is top of mind, too.

ANT COLONY LEADERSHIP STYLE

Chouinard's leadership style is hands off. He says this style made sense after hearing an analogy from a Stanford researcher who studied ant colonies and "found that they don't have bosses, everyone knows what their job is and they get it done." Chouinard says, "Compare that with dictatorship; it takes tremendous effort. Instead we hire motivated young independent people and leave them alone." Chouinard says that many companies have studied their culture and want to follow suit; but he says, "It won't work unless you begin with the first employee.

A psychologist has studied our employees and says they are so independent they'd be unemployable anywhere else." Chouinard chuckles with pride on the podcast, knowing that doesn't matter; those employees aren't going anywhere. This leadership style allows him to take off every June through November for fishing in Wyoming. And when he's away, he's away. He says he might call in three times in the five months.

REPLACE THINGS WITH KNOWLEDGE AND TECHNIQUE

Using his "the more you know, the less you need" philosophy while fly fishing taught Chouinard the vale of simplicity, and he says he caught more fish than he's ever caught in his life. "The hundreds of thousands of fly patterns, colors, shapes are totally unnecessary. You can replace all of that with knowledge and technique. That was a good lesson for me. The hardest thing in the world is to simplify your life because everything pulls you to be more and more complex. If we are forced or we decide to go to a more simple life, it's not going to be an impoverished life. It'll be a really rich [life]." Podcast host Raz reports that "While endless growth may not be Chouinard's thing, Patagonia had their best year yet in 2015 with a quarter billion dollars." Chouinard's leadership style and ideals about challenging consumer consumption while protecting the planet have made him the type of businessman he *knew* he needed to be. No business degree required. Just mindful business.

C.E.'OM: AETNA CEO MARK BERTOLINI

One high-profile corporate C.E.'Om who is making a major impact by leading with mindfulness is Aetna CEO Mark Bertolini. I interviewed Bertolini in December 2017. His full story is featured in an article I wrote for Huffington Post titled "Mindfulness is Aetna CEO's Prescription for Success." Bertolini leads Aetna's 49,000 employees from a place of calm, compassion, and mindfulness that he arrived at only after recovering from a near-death ski accident that left him on seven different narcotics and pondering the fact that he couldn't go on in pain both mentally and physically. Yoga and meditation felt a bit too New Age, but Bertolini (who no longer had the physical ability to do his preferred running and weightlifting) tried craniosacral therapy, yoga, and meditation because he was at the point of having to be open-minded to get some relief. He says it saved his life. He was able to get off all medication and become a new version of himself.

BRINGING MINDFULNESS AND WELLNESS TO 49,000 EMPLOYEES

Soon after becoming CEO, Bertolini began Aetna's mindfulness-based wellness programs with a study. He says, "We measured heart rate variability to establish stress levels for approximately 250 employees. We put them into quintiles and the highest quintile of stress was spending upwards of $2,000 a year more on health care costs than the average. We invested in 12 weeks of yoga and mindfulness training in a set of practices established with eMindful and Gary Kraftsow of the *American Viniyoga Institute*. At the end of that study we saw dramatic drops in heart rate variability and an increase in presenteeism and productivity. The employee's journals were the most compelling part; they led us on our discovery to see exactly what factors were causing high-stress levels." The study and journals showed that stressors for employees focused mainly on their pay and benefits. To address this issue, in 2015 Aetna raised the minimum wage for its employees, increasing wages for more than 5,700 employees, while enhancing health benefits for thousands of employees at the same time. Bertolini says, "We decided that we needed to raise our minimum wage from $12 to $16 hour, and we saw that this change directly impacted their health benefits. So, we agreed to erase that health benefits cost if they agreed to take care of themselves through company programs and health initiatives. We call this the *Aetna Social Compact*." They also learned that those stressors were causing anxiety and lack of sleep. Bertolini is an advocate of a good night's sleep and wanted to show the importance of getting at least seven hours of sleep per night, so Aetna began incentivizing employees to sleep better. For every 20 nights that employees slept those 7 hours, they would receive $25, and could receive up to $300 over the course of the year for this incentive. The program was completely voluntary and on the honor system, and more than 15,000 employees have taken advantage of this incentive over the past three years.

THE VALUE OF INVESTING IN GOOD HEALTH

Bertolini says, "It's critical to invest in the human machine in trying to eliminate stressors to build resiliency. In our world, the only thing that's going to happen with change is that it's going to get faster and the organizations that have capable people need to have them be resilient in order to be able to make it and change, adapt and move forward. Part of creating change in an organization is creating this resiliency." Aetna built a Mindfulness Center at its corporate headquarters in Hartford, Connecticut because they wanted to have a place for people to practice mindfulness inside the building. They even have some pet therapy, where pet therapists come in with animals for employees to spend time with. But Bertolini notes that although the center is new, Aetna has had a Chief Mindfulness Officer (Andy Lee) for more than three years. Lee's focus is to continue to enhance the mindfulness programs for Aetna employees, while also promoting the use of mindfulness programs among Aetna's customers.

It's likely no coincidence that the Aetna stock price has multiplied more than six times since Bertolini has been at the helm. Not only has he focused on his own health and wellness, but he's an authentic advocate for all 49,000 employees. As for his chronic pain, he describes how the power of breath allows him to move through it daily. Bertolini still suffers from neuropathic pain in his left arm. Since a long session of meditation isn't always an option on his schedule, he can tap into a meditative state quickly, even in just a few deep, well-intentioned breaths. He says, "I still have intense pain from my left ear to left fingertips most of the day, but when it becomes a distraction I can take one deep breath and much like prana (the Sanskrit word for breath, life force), pull the pain up, then exhale a breath out while pushing the pain out. One more breath in and then out releases the pain. That's my personal technique, realizing that by being present and understanding that my pain is actually not in my arm, it's in my spine looking for feedback from my arm. When I use breath in a way to push my pain out, I can eliminate the vast majority of the discomfort." Bertolini can sound more like a yoga teacher now than a high-powered, high-profile CEO. He spends quite a bit of effort speaking publicly and sharing the benefits of mindfulness because it's had such a profoundly positive impact on his life and it's a big part of who he today as a leader. If Bertolini can manage his chronic pain from his desk like that with a few well-intentioned deep breaths, imagine what *you* can begin to control with breath at your desk.[62]

The technology sector seems to be particularly open to the idea of mindfulness and meditation. It *is* the best antidote to our tech-driven lives. The following three C.E.'Oms have done impactful work and continue to lead the way in showing the corporate sector the value of mindfulness in business. These three C.E.'Om's are also connected with each other: Chade-Meng Tan (former Google engineer, and reator of Google's Search Inside Yourself program, the book *Search Inside Yourself*, and the Search Inside Yourself Leadership Institute), Peter Bostelmann (former business program delivery manager and now director of Mindfulness at SAP, which is now the largest client of Cheng-Made Tan's Search Inside Yourself organization), and Bill Duane (a former Google engineer, he attended Search Inside Yourself at Google and is now a longtime well-being expert, organizational consultant, and student of Buddhism).

C.E.'OM: FORMER GOOGLE ENGINEER CHADE-MENG TAN

Let's start with Chade-Meng Tan because he's the OG! (urban slang for trailblazer or innovator). Tan was an early Google engineer (Employee #107), and after being there for several years, he wanted to share his desire for happiness and mindfulness. He developed curriculum for Google called Search Inside Yourself. His advocacy for mindfulness led to him to a new full-time position: Google's "Jolly Good Fellow." His Search Inside Yourself program (a mindfulness-based emotional intelligence course) became a best-selling book in 2012. Tan left Google and in 2013 launched a nonprofit called the Search Inside Yourself Leadership Institute, where the program is now open source to other corporations. Tan is on a mission to contribute to world peace. In his 2010 TED talk, Tan says that the Search Inside Yourself program worked at Google because Google thrives on idealism, and because of that, compassion is organic and widespread. He explains why a company culture of compassion fits at Google and how you can make it fit at your organization too:

- Expressions of corporate compassion follow a pattern at Google. Tan explains how because of their highly independent work model, a very small group of people can take an idea or initiative and simply start something grassroots. They don't ask for permission. Eventually, if it's for the greater good, it will be noticed, and if it's successful and big enough, it can then become official. Example: The largest Google community event happened where "Googlers" around the world volunteered in their local communities. It was organized and launched with just three people, but the idea of participating resonated far and wide; it got so big and so popular that it became official.

- There are several philanthropic initiatives that all came about because of a very small group of passionate and mindful employees. "There was so much organic social action happening around Google that the company decided to form a social responsibility team just to support these efforts. This idea came from two Googlers who wrote their own job descriptions and volunteered themselves for the job. It wasn't formed as some grand corporate strategy, it was two people saying, 'Let's do this' and the company said, 'Yes.'"

- Tan says, "Googlers find compassion to be fun *and* there are real business benefits of compassion. It creates highly effective business leaders with two common traits: humility and ambition. They are ambitious for the greater good, it's not ego driven. Another benefit is it creates an inspiring workforce. Employees mutually inspire each other towards greater good, the atmosphere is energetic and vibrant where people admire and respect each other."

Tan's case study at Google is a great example of *doing* something when you know it's going to help people. It's like the adage that it's easier to ask forgiveness than permission. If it's your calling to speak up and share your mindfulness, do it![63]

C.E.'OM: SAP'S DIRECTOR OF MINDFULNESS PROGRAM, PETER BOSTELMANN

Peter Bostelmann was working at the Palo Alto, California office of SAP (a German-based multinational publicly traded software company with nearly 90,000 employees) in 2012 when he began dreaming of bringing his personal mindfulness practice to SAP. He had two friends at the Germany headquarters who were also mindfulness advocates, and he began talking with them about the idea. They ended up testing with small pilot programs in Palo Alto, and it resonated. Chade-Meng Tan came to SAP to speak to an audience of hundreds of interested people at SAP. As the idea began to scale through other pilot programs, Bostelmann chose Tan's Search Inside Yourself program to be the official program at SAP globally. It's been so successful that it turned into a new full-time position for Bostelmann, who moved from business delivery manager to director of Mindfulness Program at SAP. SAP also became Search Inside Yourself Institute's biggest client.

MINDFULNESS IS CONTAGIOUS

Similar to Tan, Bostelmann was just one person within a huge organization who was passionate about mindfulness and made it happen from the ground up. He experienced great benefits from his own practice but had never talked about it at work, until he realized that it was important to share the wealth of knowledge because his colleagues would also deeply benefit in from the self-awareness and practice. SAP now has a waitlist of 5,000 people signed up for their workshops and teacher trainings. It sounds like people are crawling out of the woodwork to get involved because either they want in on a new practice or they want to deepen their practice by attending the teacher training. In his "How to Bring Mindfulness to a Company" talk in 2016, Bostelmann describes how you can sell a mindfulness program to your organization:

- Find someone who has both business and mindfulness background because they need to sell the idea to employees and executives. This takes drive, persistence, and courage, and it's helpful to think big from the beginning. SAP created mindfulness ambassadors and volunteers globally.

- Create a specific pitch for your organization that will resonate with the needs and goals of the company. You cannot have a one-size-fits-all approach. Link the pitch to objectives that are meaningful to your company and show how mindfulness will help reach their goals.

- Speak from potential enhancement perspective rather than speaking about curing deficiencies. Meditation is usually part of a wellness or health department, but Bostelmann says, "If you want to attract the alpha male and female, they define themselves by their capacity to perform; they're not attracted by the idea of health problems. If you approach it as an enhancement program: i.e. increases cognitive capacity, proven by science, increases leadership and social skills . . . then people get interested. Choose your language carefully, talk about it in a way that's compelling." He shares an anecdote about the importance of lingo. He

worked as a coach and recommended meditation exercises to a client who became offended;
she wasn't interested in "that hippie stuff." A
few weeks later he suggested they do "attention
training" exercise. She enthusiastically agreed.
They were, of course, the same exercise. "She
overcame her bias because she related to the
science-based language. Language within
the business context should not be esoteric,
religious or spiritual. You want to attract the
skeptics too. Frame it as scientifically proven
mental strength training."

- Get strong testimonials; when a German VP
  of sales at SAP says the course can change
  your life, that helps. He recommended it in
  the office and people were curious.

Bostelmann has grown the program and now has a
team. They have meaningful data that he shares publicly
at conferences to illustrate the value of mindfulness in
business for employees and for the health of large organizations. From grassroots to a global mindfulness practice, it has become an integral part of the culture at SAP.
The investment is paying off in many ways that include
less absenteeism and higher well-being as well as better engagement, focus, and trust. Bostelmann hopes to

inspire other individuals to start like he did and for other companies to consider the SAP data and bring mindfulness into their global organizations.[64]

C.E.'OM: FORMER GOOGLE ENGINEER BILL DUANE

Bill Duane was a Google engineer who took the *Search Inside Yourself* course in 2007 and then also studied mindfulness-based stress relief in 2008. Like Tan, he transitioned from engineer to become a Google Well-Being expert and a mindfulness and organizational consultant (for Google and then on his own for other big corporate brands). He worked twelve years at Google and now has ten years of consulting experience in healthcare, manufacturing, finance, telecom, and media with studies in neuroscience, team effectiveness, mindfulness, and well-being science. Duane is one of the leading experts in mindfulness within the corporate arena. In April 2018, I interviewed Duane. Here's some of his advice on bringing mindfulness to business professionals.

MEET PEOPLE WHERE THEY ARE

"Your Type A client's key constraint in life is going to be time. If you come at them saying, 'Hey, you should devote time to this thing (mindfulness or meditation), that on the surface appears to them to be nonproductive; it's a nonstarter. Instead, we need to explain the good news that these skills offer in regard to self-awareness, self-regulation, and connection, how they're good for cognitive performance, strategic visioning, and stress reduction. In order to get in the door, you have to understand the group of humans that you're dealing with and help them solve a problem, and ideally this should be a business problem. You can't lead with information where the client has no context to understand it. If someone wants to work on these skills, it's useful to pick something very specific and then use that as the lever. If you tie it to a specific problem that they desperately want to solve, they'll be willing to invest time in self-awareness and meditation."

EXECS NEED TO UNDERSTAND THEIR EXECUTIVE PRESENCE

"In terms of self-awareness for Type A, one of the things that leads to the doorway opening is executive presence; someone who is clueless about how they're being received does not have good executive presence." Duane recommends the "Johari Window" technique for helping executives better understand their relationship with themselves and others and says that the concept helps in developing the self-awareness for good executive presence.

OVERTIME ISN'T ALWAYS PRODUCTIVE

"When I teach, I share that the ROI for time at work becomes neutral and then decreases depending on where you are. There are times when the most productive thing to do is stop working . . . but that feels radically unsafe. The reason we blow past the ROI on time at work and it becomes neutral and then negative is because we lack the self-awareness of 'I'm making mistakes.' For me, I know the flavor of mental exhaustion and when I start tasting that flavor of experience, I know I'm going to make terrible decisions, gonna piss people off and ending up having to make good. You know the quote? (by ["Justified" character] Raylan Givens): 'If you run into an asshole in the morning, you ran into an asshole. If you run into assholes all day, you're the asshole.' Without self-awareness you'd actually misplace the source of it."

THE BEST PROGRAMS ARE THE ONES YOU DO

"With mindfulness and meditation, we have 'medicine' that works and yet the vast majority of people won't do it. That's why the best well-being programs are the ones you do. Whatever practice it is, if you're doing it even if it may not be as effective and you may be leaving a lot of potential for well-being on the table—if you're doing something, it's great and it may be a path toward something deeper."

Duane's life changed while he was working at Google in 2008 and dealing with an intense job along with the stress of his father's heart issues and subsequent death. Duane says, "I was taking the (mindfulness-based stress relief course when my father died in 2008, which was a massive inflection point. It was the overall, ambient stress that got me willing to check mindfulness out," and then seeing the positive effect it had during this difficult time made him consider doing it full time. Duane says, "There's no way I would have considered meditation had I not been promoted far beyond my comfort level and had my dad also not died. Tibetans say 'May you have the appropriate amount of difficulty.' Without the appropriate amount of difficulty you don't get knocked out of [your] comfort zone, particularly if you have a lot of privilege—either wealth, gender, race. If you have the ability to insulate yourself from reality, you lose these opportunities. There's a training that needs to happen around adversity and how to deal with it. If you can always buy your way out of discomfort, you don't have that opportunity." Duane is currently studying to be a Buddhist teacher.[65]

C.E.'OM: SALESFORCE CEO MARC BENIOFF

One more C.E.'Om from the tech space. If you're in the business sector, you're probably familiar with

Salesforce, the publicly traded cloud computing software company. Salesforce CEO Marc Benioff is known for being a long-time meditation and mindfulness advocate and practitioner. It's said that Steve Jobs had a big influence on Benioff appreciating meditation. Steve Jobs would likely be proud of how Benioff has brought that philosophy directly to his 7,000 employees in the new Salesforce headquarters in San Francisco. Benioff didn't come up with all of the design ideas on his own, though; he brought in Vietnamese Zen master Thich Nhat Hanh and an entourage of thirty monks to consult. The new Salesforce building stands out from the outside because it's the tallest skyscraper in San Francisco, but it's unique on the inside as well because Benioff built meditation rooms on each floor along with mindfulness zones. He's hoping the time spent in meditation will result in more innovative thinking. Benioff says via a *Business Insider* article: "There's a mindfulness zone where employees can put their phones into a basket or whatever, and go in to an area where there's quietness. I think this is really important to cultivating innovation in your company. You can go there and not have kind of a chit-chat going on in your mind for a few moments. That's more important today because we're in this always-on economy."[66]

MAKING SPACE WITH MONKS FOR MEDITATION AT THE OFFICE

Benioff also recently invited the monks and nuns from Plum Village (a French monastic community) to the annual 170,000-person Salesforce conference. They offer mindfulness and meditation techniques to all the attendees from a big tent outside the conference. Having such accessible meditation spaces for employees to breathe and find a few minutes of unplugged time adds real value at Salesforce on so many levels: quick energy and perspective shifts as well as boosts of creativity and clarity that will no doubt lead to more better communication, relationships, and collaboration. Dedicating space to the idea of mindfulness is certainly admirable and speaks volumes about the priority that Benioff places on employee workplace wellness.[67,68]

C.E.'OM: LT. COL. JANNELL MACAULAY, U.S. AIR FORCE

Lieutenant Colonel Jannell MacAulay, U.S. Air Force, had simultaneously been an Air Force pilot, the wife of a serviceman who also gets deployed, mother of two children, and a squadron commander. She's proud to be the first person to speak openly about bringing meditation and mindfulness to the Air Force as a tool for leadership and performance. I spoke with MacAulay in April 2018 about how this came about and the legacy she leaves as she retires. She says, "A critique I often get is that mindfulness will make the military soft, when in reality it gives us our edge; it keeps us on the edge because it helps us live in the moment. Greatness happens in the moment."

SELF-AWARENESS FIRST

MacAulay has led a life full of incredible successes that would send most people into a tailspin, but she found herself in a place about eight years ago where she didn't feel successful. She felt as if she had lost herself. It was during a particularly stressful time; her husband was deployed, she was working full-time as a leader and a pilot, and she had a two-year-old child. She began to ask herself questions like, "What's wrong? Why is success so hard? Why is life so challenging? How can I sustain this?" She realized that she had achieved everything she'd ever wanted; she fulfilled a childhood dream and became a pilot, she received her PhD, and led a squadron, but she still felt as if she was falling short daily. She wasn't being the best version of herself. She began to write it off as just part of aging and as a result of parenting and professional responsibilities. But that didn't sit well with MacAulay; she knew better. She has an undergraduate degree in biology and a master's degree in exercise physiology. She was ready for a full self-transformation to get to a point where she could sustain her success and begin to feel good again.

She tried yoga and says, "It became this space where I could just be me—not anyone's boss or mom. In the military especially, and in business, we can suffer from 'decision fatigue.' In yoga nobody was asking me questions, nobody needed anything from me, there were no expectations tied to yoga." She found that breath off the mat also helped her make better decisions. Along with yoga and the idea of silence and solitude came eating healthy whole food and finding time for self-reflection. Everything had come back together for MacAulay; she felt strong and whole again. She says, "I personally found mindfulness and a focus on human performance to be such a powerful force in my life that that's how I wanted to lead."

EASING HER SQUADRON INTO THE IDEA OF MEDITATION

"I didn't want jump in and say to my 400-person unit, 'Hey, I meditate and now so will you.' That certainly won't work. Instead, I led by example and demonstrated those behaviors as a leader; I was present, connected, situationally aware and focused. I built trust first, which opened the door for me to then introduce yoga. Then I introduced them to the concept [of] mindfulness and living in the present, so when they were in an aircraft or an air traffic controller, they would be able to handle the stress, make better decisions and perform at higher levels." She had developed a simple practice that she called "Going to the Cloud." "It meant stepping back, taking two deep breaths (but if you need more, take more) or sometimes you may need just one deep breath. With flying, it's high stress, high speed, life-or-death things happen quickly and one single deep breath can anchor me." Fifty percent of the people MacAulay led were under age 23, so she wanted them to understand that when they felt the physical signs of stress—clammy hands, heart racing, butterflies in their stomach—that's when they should immediately "Go to the Cloud." "Then they could respond instead of react. It started there and they latched onto the term too."

MacAulay uses mindfulness as a tool for self-awareness and self-reflection. She says, "We should all understand who we are, what we believe in, and what guides us in life. I ask people, 'What are your guiding principles?' That's also where my two deep breaths in my morning began. Instead of checking email or social media, where I might feel judged or inadequate or stressed or angry and then interacting with my kids first thing while on edge, instead of reaching for my phone, I take two deep breaths and do self-reflection on my guiding principle and personal mission statement: Who Am I? Where Am I Going? It takes a while to develop, but once you have it it's your grounding in foundation. It's a powerful exercise for people. That's where I live from every day and I try to help others figure those things out too."

MINDFULNESS FOR THE WIN!

MacAulay then started introducing mindfulness at different group meetings, including once a month with all 400 in her squadron. Then at the senior staff meeting with about twenty people once a week, she'd do a minute of breathing before the meeting began to focus attention on the task at hand. She would call it a "cognitive preparation," and would always present science-based research so that the other senior staff understood the value. MacAulay could see the effects of mindfulness in concrete ways. She says, "Everyone becomes more aware of better interactions. Not only did our culture shift but performance increased; we won several awards. Five airmen were selected for officer training school out of one squadron in one year, which is unheard of. We also won 'Airfield of Year' for the entire Air Force. It wasn't because we meditated, but meditation was the pathway to high performance. It was the means for our ability to perform at high levels and perform as a team. There's still a stigma attached to yoga in the military; we tie weakness to slowing down. That's what led likely to my executive fatigue and burnout. We don't realize value in slowing down. We need to slow down, though, and that's, interestingly enough, the more courageous choice."

We're sure to hear more from Jannell MacAulay as she retires from her current job at PACE (Profession of Arms Center of Excellence) and will be writing books and continuing to speak and teach about mindfulness in business.[69]

C.E.'OM: JANICE MARTURANO, FORMER VP AT GENERAL MILLS, NOW FOUNDER OF THE INSTITUTE OF MINDFUL LEADERSHIP

Janice Marturano is another former corporate executive like Chade-Meng Tan and Bill Duane, who left corporate life to build their own mindfulness-based business. Marturano, a former vice president at General Mills for 15 years and now founder and executive director of the Institute of Mindful Leadership (since 2011) left corporate life after a very intense eighteen-month period at General Mills where she was working eighteen-hour days, seven days a week for months on end to complete an acquisition. She also suffered the loss of both of her parents during that time. "It was a perfect storm of an extraordinarily difficult time," she says in an interview with Arianna Huffington. Marturano says that there was no time to grieve for her parents because she was responsible for the jobs of 10,000 people during this acquisition. After that transaction she was sent on a retreat called "The Power of Mindfulness: An Intensive Retreat for Executives," and that changed the course of her life. She says, "We have an amazing wealth of wisdom within us, and it gets covered over by being distracted yet we have this innate capacity in our minds to reflect, to actually allow the inner wisdom to arise and to help us make those conscious choices."[70]

Marturano began to see the difference in herself as a leader after the retreat, and her colleagues saw a change, too. They wanted to bring similar changes to their lives, so Marturano shared her knowledge. Now, with the Institute of Mindful Leadership, she is dedicated to "bringing mindful leadership curriculum to people around the globe. It doesn't take a monumental shift; the small step or the small change is really important to us beginning to turn into the kind of society that we need." I asked Marturano how to best integrate mindfulness to teams who saw mindfulness as too "out there." She responded, "I have taught thousands of leaders over the past 12 years and I am often asked how to bring this to a skeptical team. First, model the behaviors of leading as a mindful leader: focused, clear, creative, and compassionate (these are the four Fundamentals of Excellence that the Institute's curricula train). Second, introduce the practices with a reputable organization that can customize the training for the culture. Finally, demystify this work by comparing it to training the innate capacities of our body. This is training for the mind." Marturano travels the globe, sharing her insights and experience about mindful leadership with a variety of organizations, from corporate to academic institutions, nonprofits, and the military.

C.E.'OM: KATE ROSS LEBLANC, CO-FOUNDER OF SAJE NATURAL WELLNESS

Kate Ross LeBlanc cofounded Saje Natural Wellness over twenty-five years ago with a passion for both the power of nature and connecting with community. Kate knows the feeling of community from growing up in her mother's fabric store on small-town Main Street in Ontario, Canada. She's had a longtime spiritual practice that is at the core of her mindful leadership, and it can be seen in their company culture, from product development to the aesthetic and vibe of the stores. Even in the age of eComm and Amazon, Kate, her husband and Saje cofounder Jean-Pierre LeBlanc, along with daughter Kiara LeBlanc (vice president of Creative) are focused on opening more storefronts. They believe that people still want and need to connect in person. I interviewed LeBlanc for Thrive Global; here's an excerpt.

AUTHENTICALLY CONNECTING WITH CONSUMERS

"One of our natural human desires is to have our lives witnessed. That's important for me to do anywhere, and as a retail company we have an opportunity to not just witness lives, but make a difference in someone's wellness through our stores. We can look our community members in the eye and ask them meaningful questions about their lives and their wellness. They can be heard. Our driving force will always be about connection, really seeing people and creating a space where community members can feel like they are part of something bigger; inspiring people to be the best version of themselves. I'm confident that when people leave their house and venture out, whether they know it or not, they are looking for connection and that's what will keep them coming back."

HER DAILY PRACTICE

Mindfulness informs the way LeBlanc approaches the world. "Empowered by that deep knowledge and understanding that we are all writing our own stories, my interaction with both community and my team members is intentional and mindful. I know I can always shift my mindset, learn from something, see it on a different dimension as opposed to getting jostled around. I've developed my own breathing and visualization techniques for any situation where I feel my emotions in a non-supportive way. I take time to close my eyes, breathe, visualize what it is that I want to manifest. Within thirty seconds or a minute, I shift and have a connection with my higher self. I don't even realize that I do it any longer, my breath, visualization and energy managing is

naturally part of what I do as as I move through the day."
Saje Natural Wellness is based in Vancouver with 71
locations across North America and 1,200 team members, and has plans for retail expansion.[71]

C.E.'OM: OPRAH WINFREY

Anyone who knows me knows that I've been deeply
inspired by Oprah for decades and credit her television
show back in 1992 for giving me the inspiration to launch
my Moisture Jamzz business. I continue to be in awe of her
work ethic, creativity and meaningful success that stems
from her intention to bring out the best in people. Oprah
Winfrey is the epitome of a *C.E.'Om*. It's hard to fathom
the extent of change and innovation that has been a direct
result of her inspiring, educating, and supporting such a
diverse audience for so long. She's all about positive energy,
human connection, and mindful intention in business and
in life. She's shown us that we are all more alike than we
are different. Her mix of business savvy and drive to connect and inspire people to live their best life has allowed
her to grow and scale in different mediums but with the
same hope of creating impactful and meaningful work and
art. After four decades in the broadcasting industry and
as a mindful entrepreneur, Oprah has touched, changed,
and inspired millions of lives in a way that's authentic and

heartfelt—all the while, becoming the world's first African American female billionaire. Coincidence? I think not.

KEEN SENSE OF SELF-AWARENESS

An inspiring story that Oprah shares highlights her keen sense of self-awareness and intention even as a child. I was lucky enough to hear her share this anecdote in person recently, and she tells it slowly and mindfully because it's those "aha" moments that Oprah wants us all to tightly grasp onto. Oprah was about eight years old, sitting on a rural southern porch watching her grandmother hang laundry out to dry. Her grandmother told her to watch carefully so that when *she* did this for people, she'd know how to do it correctly. Both Oprah's mother and grand-mother were domestic workers. Oprah immediately responded, "I'm *not* going to be doing this." She *knew*. That feeling was strongly embedded into her and she moved through her life accordingly. Up against extremely challenging odds in the broadcasting industry, Oprah disrupted by unapologetically being her authentic self. Her journey is a powerful example of mindfulness, intention, transparency, and good old persistence and tenacity. Working her way up from reporter, to anchor and host of the most successful talk show ever in America for twenty-five years, she became powerful in business because she was more than the show's talent. She owned the production company for "The Oprah Winfrey Show." Her business savvy was right up there with her empathy and humility.

WHEN YOU LOVE WHAT YOU DO, YOU KEEP ON DOING IT!

After forty years of nonstop, hard work, most people would retire and relax after signing off from *that* show. Not Oprah. Thank goodness! She simultaneously ended her show while launching the OWN (Oprah Winfrey Network) television network in 2011. She has said that the new venture was a major uphill climb and more difficult than she ever imagined it could be. But again, she knew she was "called" to build a platform that would fill people's soul, building the network she felt was missing in the marketplace and sharing her deeply ingrained spirituality that she began talking about on her show long before people even knew what mindfulness meant.

On the last episode of the "The Oprah Winfrey Show," Oprah said, "I've talked to nearly 30,000 people on this show, and all 30,000 had one thing in common: They all wanted validation. . . . Understanding that one principle, that everybody wants to be heard, has allowed me to hold the microphone for you all these years with the least amount of judgment. . . . Try it with your children, your husband, your wife, your boss, your friends. Validate them. 'I see you. I hear you. And what you say matters to me.'" This lesson certainly has business applications.

Oprah exemplifies the qualities of mindfulness in business not only through her own personal climb to success but in her leadership at Harpo, OWN, and the Oprah Winfrey Girls Leadership Academy in South Africa. She walks the walk. Oprah is an outspoken meditation advocate and leads a free twenty-one-day meditation series with Deepak Chopra a few times every year. On Oprah's Super Soul Conversations podcast recently, she talked with Amy Schumer about their mutual affection for meditation. Oprah said, "It's one of the most life-enhancing things I've ever done. The ultimate in going in." She's also an avid intention setter. Oprah has said that she will not start a project, a meeting, or even phone call without having a clear intention of what's going to transpire. She's an activist, philanthropist, actress, producer, CEO, leader, entrepreneur, and whatever else she decides she wants to be! She is tireless and on a mission to create meaningful work that continues to inspire and change people for the greater good. She will no doubt leave a never-ending legacy.[72]

Speaking of Oprah, one last example of a brand that is very recently innovating with a new purpose and focus on wellness is the company formerly called Weight Watchers. The 55-year-old company is now known simply as WW, with the tagline "Wellness That Works." Oprah is a recent investor in the brand, and the influence that she has in regard to mindfulness as a big part of well-being aligns perfectly with the new philosophy of WW, which focuses on wellness rather than weight loss. That's a big shift for a big organization; they're listening to the marketplace. *Time* magazine named WW President and CEO Mindy Grossman on its list of the 50 Most Influential People in Health Care for 2018 as she is helping to redefine wellness. This is one more brand that sees the SOS for a new way to live in 2018 and beyond. If we don't take the time to focus on our health, we're going to have to spend time healing from ailments that develop from overextending ourselves with constant digital connection. Grossman is quoted in a *Forbes* article: "The vernacular of wellness has definitely evolved. The way we think about it is very holistic. It's what you put in your body, how you move your body and how your mind supports your efforts, but the big thing that has changed is people want to define what healthy is, too. We've done a lot of consumer work over the past number of years and synthesized it down into a number of things that have really influenced how we're moving forward. And people want inspiration. It's not just information. There's too much conflicting noise happening right now. So if you can both give people the information and inspiration then, what we like to say is, healthy is the new skinny and that's very empowering for people. We want to help people be the healthiest version of themselves."[73]

While these and many other C.E.'Oms have made incredible traction and set admirable examples, there's still a lot of work to be done with bringing mindfulness and well-being to the business sector. But there's hope now because science, awareness, conversation, data, and funding all lie behind initiatives now. We just need to keep pushing them forward, one deep breath at a time.

7

THE STUDENT BECOMES THE MASTER: OWNING YOUR BREATH

*The mind is the king of the senses, and
the breath is the king of the mind.*
—B. K. S. IYENGAR

You've got this! You're ready to *Breathe like a Boss* and
live in the energy and mindset that will bring you
whatever you have your (positive) mind set on. Breath is
energy, and it will offer you a new level of clarity, confidence, creativity, connection, and productivity. Breath gives
you access to your brain and emotions that offer you a new
sense of leverage in reaching your goals. It's science! How
you think and feel is a choice—a very important choice.

Breathing Like a Boss—mindful breath powered by
personalized strategic positive thoughts and intentions

in the moment when you need it most—that is true empowerment for success. There's so much to learn from experts, teachers, inspirational books, apps, podcasts, classes, events, conferences, conversations . . . but then *you've* got to bring it home and make it your own. Become a master. Owning your breath in your unique way makes it exponentially more effective and empowering because you never have to wait for anyone or anything to use the power of breath. Own your breath and own your peace. Therein lies the magic. You are your best teacher, healer, and motivator. The more you practice, the more inner strength you'll build so that the best version of yourself becomes your default mode.

Now you know how to:

- Be more self-aware and notice your thoughts and emotions.

- Choose to take control of your thoughts and emotions with breath and make the mind–body connection.

- Close your eyes and go inward.

- Visualize your dream business scenarios.

- Develop your intentions for mindful business.

- Create your own mantras to gain inner strength and confidence.

- Use different breath techniques—3DB, lion's breath, bee breath, alternate nostril breathing, breath retention, ujjayi. Mix and match them with the multipliers listed above.

- Be self-aware of your screen time, mental fatigue, and brain fog, and manage your digital wellness.

- Turn your morning routine into a powerful ritual.

- Fuel your brain/body with nourishing beverages and food.

- Build a new relationship with time and timing.

- Be an inspirational C.E.'Om.

I've felt the benefits of breath firsthand for thirty years now, and it sometimes feels so simple that it's silly: how a better state of mind is always only 3DB away. When I share the secret sauce, the feedback warms my heart. It's game changing. Breath is nothing short of miraculous. Breath *is* meditation—3DB at a time. Breathing mindfully is something you do for yourself, but it ends up being a gift for those you work with, too. It helps the greater good to share energy that's positive because it's contagious. Use your breath a bit every single day; it wants to help. Power it up with your thoughts and intentions for supercharged energy that is laser focused. Consider breath as much a part of your day as food and water. You need it to nourish and sustain you, and to bring out the best in you. Food. Water. Breath. Success.

Getting started is so simple, so keep it simple. There are no barriers; just breathe mindfully more often. The fact that you'll be using breath in under sixty seconds makes this new practice sustainable. No preparation required; just that new level of self-awareness. When you find yourself reacting to a moment that requires all you've got inside yourself to hold your tongue or to decide that you will *not* give up or that you *will* move forward, that's when your breath has the most impact. You'll recognize when your body is in stress mode; you'll acknowledge it and breathe. You'll silently talk yourself through something in a new way that feels empowering rather than defeating. You now have the tools to get your mind and body working in partnership.

We all experience business through the lens of our past experiences. Breath is an equalizer. It's a connector. It helps us be less judgmental and more compassionate so that we can work with gratitude and appreciation for our colleagues at all levels. We can't control other people, but we can try to relate to them and understand them better. The Socrates quote "Be kind because everyone you meet is fighting a hard battle" is certainly relevant in business. You don't know what experience someone brings to the table with them, but breath will bring an open mind for you to work mindfully and make people feel at ease and valued.

DON'T WAIT FOR A CRISIS

Two of the C.E.'Oms featured (Bertolini and Duane) admitted that they never would have gravitated toward breath, meditation, or mindfulness had it not been for their personal crisis. And then it massively transformed their life. Getting to a point of desperation is often what it takes before trying something that seems so outside your wheelhouse. But don't wait. The only thing that is constant is change. Breath will help you adapt to constant change.

CHANGE OFTEN BEGINS IN THE BUSINESS SECTOR

If we can all bring breath to work with us, the business sector can lead the way for a major shift in mindfulness in business. Business has transformed so much of our behavior and lifestyle, especially over the past ten years; it can do the same with breath and mindfulness. As you become your own source of empowerment with mindful breathing, you'll notice that you feel more to connected to people again. Your mind is more open because your eyes, ears, and heart are more open. You may find yourself asking your colleagues and business partners, "How can I help you?" You'll have more to give. More opportunities will come to you as well. Commit to taking charge of your thoughts and emotions. Choose to be the person that you want to be in business—use everything you've got inside to give it your all; follow your dreams; make an impact; and change, build, or create something special. Tap into your full potential for success. You are more connected to what matters now—yourself—and that leads to better connecting with others. Success in business is based on relationships, and breath is the connector to producing the energy and mindset to build successful relationships.

> *Growth and comfort do not coexist.*
> — GINNY ROOMETTE

I've saved one last application for *Breathing Like a Boss* until the end because so many people are frequently stuck in the same place: their comfort zone. If you're holding yourself back for the sake of comfort or feeling content, you're limiting yourself. I tend to be a creature of habit, so I'm speaking from experience. I will try to control situations so that I can stay in my comfort zone, but (I'm still learning) the best things happen when we take a leap of faith. Breath is the best tool to support you in taking new risks and doing things even though they're uncomfortable. Breath brings inner strength to your "new" zone, and often it doesn't take too long before you can find comfort in what was just unknown. Keep taking those leaps powered by your strategic thoughts and mindful intentions. Breathe them *into* something amazing—outside of your comfort zone!

A few years into my business, I got an exciting invitation to sell our Moisture Jamzz products on QVC. It was something I'd hoped for at every trade show. As I discussed the logistics of the products, the buyer casually mentioned something about the process of *me* selling on the air. Wait, what? I hadn't thought about that part. I didn't want to be on air. That was so outside my comfort zone. I liked working behind the camera. I majored in broadcasting and journalism and interned in newsrooms all through college, but I was behind the scenes—floor manager or holding the mic for the "person on the street" interviews, getting the soundbites—not being on camera. This QVC situation was an incredible opportunity, but I didn't want the stress of being on live international television. I told the buyer that I much preferred if our products go on one of their beauty-themed shows where there were occasionally products being sold by a professional host or salesperson. Although these were much shorter segments, it made me more comfortable having someone else do the talking on air. The buyer said that having the entrepreneur on was *always* better for sales. I decided not to believe her and proceeded with their purchase order (which was a custom-made product for QVC that I could not resell to another client) and having the host sell for us because that was comfortable. It wasn't brain surgery; the host could sell a pair of moisturizing gloves and moisturizer, right? The buyer reluctantly agreed but asked that I be there at QVC in the green room during the on-air presentation. We sat together and watched until I couldn't take it—after a couple of minutes I couldn't hold back, "What's happening? She [the host] isn't telling the viewers about this or that, and she's not describing it correctly. She forgot to say all those little details I had mentioned." The coveted opportunity had been wasted, and I was beside myself. I was no longer comfortable in what I thought was my comfort zone. I had to take the leap! The buyer obviously knew what she was doing. She said, "Nobody ever has the same enthusiasm or insight as the entrepreneur." Lesson learned. Speak up, and do what you have to do to get to where you want to go. When opportunities arise, even if you *can* control certain aspects, maybe you shouldn't if it will be limiting success. Thankfully, she let me come back. It was an important lesson on learning to take opportunities even if they're intimidating, because with breath, there will be a new level of comfort in any situation. You are ready for something bigger; step outside your current zone. *Breathe Like a Boss.*

It may sound cliché but it's true: *you* are your best teacher now. You'll see how breath can be a source of support like never before. Breathe like you mean it. As Bill Duane says, the best program is one that you'll *do*. Don't get hung up on the label or the details of your new practice. Call it whatever you want—just breathe. The results of your breath practice will speak for themselves. If you haven't experienced an extended feeling of "energized calm," you're in for a nice surprise.

Business is complicated.

Breath is simple.

You can breathe into something.

You can breathe through something.

You can breathe something out.

Just breathe, deeply and mindfully.

Breathe to succeed.

Everything you need to take yourself into next-level success is within you. You know what you need to do. Breathe *into that*. You know what you need to change. Breathe *through that*. You know what you need to let go of. Breathe *that out*. Breath is the vehicle. Where will you go? The choice is *yours*!

ENDNOTES

INTRODUCTION

1. Cerf, Morgan. "Neuroscientists Have Identified How Exactly a Deep Breath Changes Your Mind." November 19, 2007. Quartzy.qz.com. *https://quartzy.qz.com/1132986/neuroscientists-have-identified-how-exactly-a-deep-breath-changes-your-mind/*.

2. Axe, Josh. "10 Ways Chronic Stress Is Killing Your Quality of Life." DrAxe.com. *https://draxe.com/10-ways-chronic-stress-is-killing-your-quality-of-life/*.

3. Feifer, Jason. "Lessons Learned from Interviewing the Editor in Chief of Entrepreneur Magazine, Jason Feifer." LinkedIn. May 5, 2018. *www.linkedin.com/pulse/lessons-learned-from-interviewing-editor-chief-magazine-mark-metry/*.

CHAPTER 1

4. Goh, Crystal. "Your Breath Is Your Brain's Remote Control." Mindful.Org. February 16, 2017. *www.mindful.org/breath-brains-remote-control/*.

5. Ben-Shahar, Tal. "The Wonders of Deep Breathing." Spirituality & Health. March 16, 2014. *https://spiritualityhealth.com/articles/2014/03/06/wonders-deep-breathing*.

6. "How to Detoxify Your Body." Go Methodology. January 24, 2017. *www.gomethodology.com/blog/2017/1/24/how-to-detoxify-your-body*.

7. Boncompagni, Tatiana, and Andrew D. Huberman. "Want a Better Workout? Just Breathe." *The New York Times.* January 4, 2018. *www.nytimes.com/2018/01/04/nyregion/want-a-better-workout-just-breathe.html*.

8. AZquotes. *www.azquotes.com/quote/868839*.

9. Tjan, Anthony K. "How Leaders Become Self-Aware." *Harvard Business Review.* July 19, 2012. *https://hbr.org/2012/07/how-leaders-become-self-aware*.

10. Winkler, Becky. "Share New Study Shows Nice Guys Finish First." American Marketing Association. *www.amanet.org/training/articles/new-study-shows-nice-guys-finish-first.aspx?pcode=XCRP*.

11. Eurich, Tascha. "What Self-Awareness Really Is (and How to Cultivate It)." HBR.org. January 4, 2018. *https://hbr.org/2018/01/what-self-awareness-really-is-and-how-to-cultivate-it*.

12. Bach, David. "Rewire Your Body's Stress Reaction." Itunes.com. January 2, 2018. *https://itunes.apple.com/us/podcast/neuronfire/id1261623813?mt=2*.

CHAPTER 2

13. Reynolds, Susan. "Happy Brain, Happy Life." *Psychology Today.* August 2, 2011. *www.psychologytoday.com/us/blog/prime-your-gray-cells/201108/happy-brain-happy-life*.

Endnotes

14. Salvi, C., E. Bricolo, S. L. Franconeri, J. Kounios, and M. Beeman. "Sudden Insight Is Associated with Shutting Out Visual Inputs." PubMed.gov. December 22, 2015. *www.ncbi.nlm.nih.gov/pubmed/26268431.*

15. Tan, Chade-Meng. Search Inside Yourself. GoodReads.com. *www.goodreads.com/author/show/5285801.Chade_Meng_Tan.*

16. Sathyanarayana Rao, T. S., M. R. Asha, K. S. Jagannatha Rao, and P. Vasudevaraju. "The BioChemistry of Belief." NCBI NIH. October 2009. *www.ncbi.nlm.nih.gov/pmc/articles/PMC2802367/.*

17. Amortegui, Jessica. "Why Finding Meaning at Work Is More Important than Feeling Happy." FastCompany.com. June 6, 2014. *www.fastcompany.com/3032126/how-to-find-meaning-during-your-pursuit-of-happiness-at-work.*

18. Rosenbaum, Steven, and Tony Hsieh. "The Happiness Culture: Zappos Isn't a Company — It's a Mission." FastCompany.com. June 4, 2010. *www.fastcompany.com/1657030/happiness-culture-zappos-isnt-company-its-mission.*

19. Read. Think. Act. "We're in the People Business." *https://readthinkact.com/were-in-the-people-business/.*

20. Chouinard, Yvon. "Patagonia B corp." Patagonia.com. *www.patagonia.com/b-lab.html.*

21. Abrams, Sandy, and Yancey Strickler. "Small Crowdfunding Donations Have Large Economic Impact." HuffingtonPost.com. August 9, 2016. *www.huffingtonpost.com/sandy-abrams/small-crowdfunding-donati_b_11355180.html.*

22. Ferriss, Tim, and Astro Teller. "Tim Ferriss Podcast." YouTube.com. October 29, 2015. *www.youtube.com/watch?v =WQxBr9fQjhY*.

23. Greenberg, Melanie. "Why Some Stress Is Good For You." *Psychology Today*. December 18, 2016. *www.psychologytoday .com/us/blog/the-mindful-self-express/201612/why-some-stress -is-good-you*.

CHAPTER 3

24. Rifkin, Rachael, and John Luckovich. "How Shallow Breathing Affects Your Whole Body." Headspace.com. *www.headspace .com/blog/2017/08/15/shallow-breathing-whole-body/*.

25. Walton, Alice G. "Science Illuminates Why Slow Breathing Calms the Mind." *Forbes*. March 31, 2017. *www.forbes.com/ sites/alicegwalton/2017/03/31/science-illuminates-why-slow- breathing-calms-the-mind/#3436ed737df6*.

26. Perry, Philip, and Christina Zelano. "How We Breathe Affects Our Thoughts and Emotions, Northwestern Researchers Find." BigThink.com. *http://bigthink.com/philip -perry/how-we-breathe-effects-our-thoughts-and-feelings -northwestern-neuroscientists-find*.

27. DiSalvo, David. "How Breathing Calms Your Brain, and Other Science-Based Benefits of Controlled Breathing." *Forbes*. November 29, 2017. *www.forbes.com/sites/daviddisalvo/ 2017/11/29/how-breathing-calms-your-brain-and-other-science -based-benefits-of-controlled-breathing/#3e0d2b752221*.

28. "Relaxation Techniques: Breath Control Helps Quell Errant Stress Response." Harvard Health Publishing. January 2015. *www.health.harvard.edu/mind-and-mood/relaxation-techniques-breath-control-helps-quell-errant-stress-response*.

29. Eisler, Melissa. "Learn the Ujjayi Breath, an Ancient Yogic Breathing Technique." Chopra.com. *https://chopra.com/articles/learn-the-ujjayi-breath-an-ancient-yogic-breathing-technique*.

30. Jeary, Tony. "Clarity: Your First Priority." Success.com. November 4, 2014.

31. Kamen, Dr. Randy. "The Transformative Power of Gratitude." Huffington Post. April 1, 2015. *www.huffingtonpost.com/randy-kamen-gredinger/the-transformative-power-_2_b_6982152.html*.

CHAPTER 4

32. Cytowic, Richard E. "Your Brain on Screens." The American Interest. June 9, 2015. *www.the-american-interest.com/2015/06/09/your-brain-on-screens/*.

33. Zomorodi, Manoush. "How Boredom Can Lead to Your Most Brilliant Ideas." TED.com. April 2017. *www.ted.com/talks/manoush_zomorodi_how_boredom_can_lead_to_your_most_brilliant_ideas?language=en*.

34. Richtel, Matt, and Loren Frank. "Digital Devices Deprive Brain of Needed Downtime." *The New York Times*. August 24, 2010. *www.nytimes.com/2010/08/25/technology/25brain.html?scp=1&sq=downtime&st=cse&_r=0*.

35. Kelly, Caitlin, and Chade-Meng Tan. "O.K., Google, Take a Deep Breath." *The New York Times.* April 28, 2012. *www.nytimes.com/2012/04/29/technology/google-course-asks-employees-to-take-a-deep-breath.html.*

36. Grosse, Jessica, and Alex Soojung-Kim Pang. "4 Ways to Cure Your Technical 'Distraction Addiction.'" FastCompany.com. September 24, 2013. *www.fastcompany.com/3018102/4-ways-to-cure-your-technological-distraction-addiction.*

37. Axe, Josh. "10 Ways Chronic Stress Is Killing Your Way of Life." DrAxe.com. *https://draxe.com/10-ways-chronic-stress-is-killing-your-quality-of-life/.*

38. Price, Catherine. *How to Break Up with Your Phone: The 30-Day Plan to Take Back Your Life.* Berkeley, CA: Ten Speed Press, 2018.

39. Bach, David. "Dr. David Bach." YouTube.com. April 10, 2016. *www.youtube.com/watch?v=6pzBuiIr_4I.*

40. Huffington, Arianna. "The Great Awakening." Thrive Global. January 16, 2018. w*ww.thriveglobal.com/stories/20884-the-great-awakening.*

41. Bever, Lindsey, and Kenneth Hansraj. "'Text Neck' Is Becoming an 'Epidemic' and Could Wreck Your Spine." *The Washington Post.* November 20, 2014. *www.washingtonpost.com/news/morning-mix/wp/2014/11/20/text-neck-is-becoming-an-epidemic-and-could-wreck-your-spine/?noredirect=on&utm_term=.5719887f5846.*

42. Harris, Dan B., and Manoush Zomorodi. "Manoush Zomorodi." Stitcher.com. January 3, 2018. *www.stitcher.com /podcast/abc-news/10-happier/e/52752946.*

43. West, Harry. "All Business Is Personal: Employees Need Human Connections at Work." Entrepreneur.com. February 17, 2017. *www.entrepreneur.com/article/288623.*

44. Ursey, Lawton. "Your Brain Unplugged: Proof That Spacing Out Makes You More Effective." *Forbes.* May 16, 2014. *www.forbes.com/sites/lawtonursrey/2014/05/16/your-brain -unplugged-proof-that-spacing-out-makes-you-more-effective/ #1ef0c072562445.*

45. McCarthy, Jeremy, Brent Bauer, Omit Sood, Paul J. Limburg, Tanya Goodin, and Thierry Malleret. "Wellness in the Age of the Smartphone." Squarespace.com. April 2018. *https:// static1.squarespace.com/static/54306a8ee4b07ea66ea32cc0/t /5ac6702ef950b7cc11212e4d/1522954292342/Wellness in the Age of the Smartphone Whitepaper.pdf.*

46. Huffington, Arianna. "The Great Awakening." Thrive Global. February 28, 2018. *https://medium.com/thrive-global /the-great-awakening-8bf08fa95eda.*

47. Google Wellbeing. *https://wellbeing.google/#_ga=2 .179902180.1735966381.1525880046-112300203 .1475248017.*

48. Center for Humane Technology, *http://humanetech.com.*

49. Crain, Esther, and Larry Rosen. "The Digital Detox That Won't Interrupt Your Life." *Men's Journal. www.mensjournal .com/health-fitness/the-digital-detox-that-won-t-interrupt-your -life-20150204/ban-devices-from-the-bedroom/.*

CHAPTER 5

50. Friedman, Ron. "Your Brain's Ideal Schedule." *Harvard Business Review.* March 26, 2015. *https://hbr.org/ideacast/2015/03/your-brains-ideal-schedule.html.*

51. Wilk, Steffanie. "Ohio State Study: Got Up on the Wrong Side of the Bed? Your Work Will Show It." OSU.EDU. April 4, 2011. *https://news.osu.edu/news/2011/04/04/newsitem3187/.*

52. Cuddy, Amy. "Your Body Language May Shape Who You Are." TED.com. June 2012. *www.ted.com/talks/amy_cuddy_your_body_language_shapes_who_you_are.*

53. Sowndharaajan, K., and Songmun Kim. "Influence of Fragrances on Human Psychophysiological Activity: With Special Reference to Human Electroencephalographic Response." NCBI NIH, November 29, 2016. *www.ncbi.nlm.nih.gov/pmc/articles/PMC5198031/.*

54. Johnson, Andrew J. "Cognitive Facilitation Following Intentional Odor Exposure." NCBI NIH, May 19, 2011. *www.ncbi.nlm.nih.gov/pmc/articles/PMC3231408/.*

55. Clear, James. "40 Years of Stanford Research Found That People with This One Quality Are More Likely to Succeed." JamesClear.com. *https://jamesclear.com/delayed-gratification.*

56. Harris, Dan B., and Daniel Pink. "'When' Can Make a Big Difference." Stitcher.com. April 4, 2018. *www.stitcher.com/podcast/abc-news/10-happier/e/53966612.*

57. Gross, Bill. "The Single Biggest Reason Why Startups Succeed." TED.com. March 2015. *www.ted.com/talks/bill_gross_the_single_biggest_reason_why_startups_succeed#t-229869.*

58. Mosconi, Dr. Lisa. "A Scientist's Guide to Eating for Brain Health." Goop.com. *https://goop.com/wellness/health /a-scientists-guide-to-eating-for-brain-health/.*

59. "Lemon Water—A Morning Tonic?" Wellness Within. September 23, 2013. *wellnesswithin.org/2013/09/lemon-water -a-morning-tonic/.*

60. Lugavere, Max. *Genius Foods: Become Smarter, Happier, and More Productive While Protecting Your Brain for Life.* New York: Harper Wave, 2018.

CHAPTER 6

61. Raz, Guy, and Yvon Chouinard. "How I Built This." NPR. December 11, 2016. *https://one.npr.org/?sharedMediaId =504852483:505017995.*

62. Abrams, Sandy, and Mark Bertolini. "Mindfulness Is Aetna CEO's Prescription for Success." HuffingtonPost. January 11, 2018. *www.huffingtonpost.com/entry/mindfulness-is-aetna -ceos-prescription-for-success_us_5a4bf577e4b0d86c803c7a1f.*

63. Tan, Chade-Meng. "Everyday Compassion at Google." TED. com. November 2010. *www.ted.com/talks/chade_meng_tan _everyday_compassion_at_google.*

64. Bostelmann, Peter. "How to Bring Mindfulness to a Global Organization." YouTube.com. April 29, 2016. *www.youtube .com/watch?v=FWDxiKP0TCs.*

65. Bill Duane, *www.billduane.com.*

66. Kim, Eugene, and Marc Benioff. "Salesforce Put a Meditation Room on Every Floor of Its New Tower Because of Buddhist Monks." BusinessInsider.com. March 7, 2016. *www.businessinsider.com/salesforce-put-a-meditation-room-on-every-floor-of-its-new-tower-2016-3.*

67. Konrad, Alex, and Marc Benioff. "How Monks Convinced Marc Benioff to Install 'Mindfulness Zones' Throughout Salesforce's New Offices." *Forbes.* March 7, 2016. *www.forbes.com/sites/alexkonrad/2016/03/07/how-monks-convinced-benioff-to-put-mindfulness-zones-in-salesforce/#3bba20c1e24467.*

68. Peterson, Becky, and Marc Benioff. "Marc Benioff Relies on These Monks for Guidance." BusinessInsider.com. November 8, 2017. *www.businessinsider.com/marc-benioff-monks-tips-for-mindful-meetings-2017-11.*

69. Jannell MacAulay, *https://jannellmacaulay.com.*

70. Huffington, Arianna, and Janice Marturano. "Huffington Post Pioneer." Institute for Mindful Leadership. April 12, 2016. *www.youtube.com/watch?v=EZrXwKKWU_E.*

71. Abrams, Sandy, and Kate Ross LeBlanc. "Retailer Goes All In on Meeting Customers 'Where They Are.'" ThriveGlobal.com. January 28, 2018. *https://medium.com/thrive-global/retailer-goes-all-in-on-meeting-customers-where-they-are-b58bcbde4b35.*

72. Winfrey, Oprah. "The Oprah Winfrey Show Finale." Oprah.com. May 25, 2011. *www.oprah.com/oprahshow/the-oprah-winfrey-show-finale_1/7.*

73. Sorveno, Chloe. "How Weight Watchers CEO Mindy Grossman Is Democratizing Wellness." June 23, 2018. *www.forbes.com/sites/chloesorvino/2018/06/23/how-weight-watchers-ceo-mindy-grossman-is-democratizing-wellness/#5be2b9547061.*

INDEX

Index

Index

Index

ACKNOWLEDGMENTS

Thank you, Jake Jacobsen (owner of Los Angeles's Center for Yoga on Larchmont in 1989) and Diana Beardsley (teacher and teacher trainer at the Center) for teaching me the all-encompassing lifestyle of yoga. Lucretia Bingham, it was your energy that made me want to try yoga in 1989. How lucky I am that our paths crossed, and I saw in you traits that I wanted to bring out in myself—the calm and cool under pressure, strategic, smart, compassionate, strong woman. I'm grateful that you credited yoga for that energy.

Deep gratitude to my second California yoga family. Thank you, Genevieve Pujalet and Suzy Nece, for your entrepreneurial labor of love in the form of the Yoga Loft, a sanctuary overlooking the Pacific ocean that is an absolutely magical and unique combo of classic yoga and "never taking it too seriously" yoga. Every deep breath I've taken at the Loft has added to my life on so many levels. It's been a second home. Thanks to all of my talented and insightful teachers there: Amanda Lee Murphy, Lane Jaffe, Justin Randolph, Shelley Williams, Christina

Holmes, David Romero, Jennifer Allen, Tiffany Maisonette, and Suzy, our chief who continues to show up and give no matter what. Talk about mindful business—you are the ultimate. You make everyone feel seen and heard and special. Love, gratitude, and Savasana to you forever, Suzy. To my original Yoga Loft tribe (Amy Schwartz, Kelly Katherine, Susan Greskovics, Glenna Stroh, Su Castro, Shelley Theodore, Anne Truscott), thank you for always being such bright lights as we watched our kids grow up and our own lives evolve. Everything is always better after a flow at the Loft. The love, support, friendship, and energy of each of you is treasured. Getting to practice almost daily next to the ballerina grace that is Robin Siegelman has been a true pleasure from our back corner spot over the past several years. I've learned so much about myself and the human spirit from that little corner. It's a privilege to breathe with all of you!

Deep gratitude to my literary agent, Joanne Brownstein Jarvi, who believed in my idea once again—eight years after I said I'd never write another book. Thanks for always telling it like is . . . and breathing and believing with me. Thank you, Michael Pye and Career Press, for understanding my vision and bringing this book to life! Thank you to the team: Kathryn Sky-Peck for the beautiful cover design that warmed my heart immediately and the meticulous editing and production by Liz Welch, Maureen Forys, and Jane Hagaman.

While breath provides me with inner strength and balance, Ron Abrams, thank you for always providing me with love and laughter. I'm happy, peaceful, and grateful when I'm breathing alongside you. Savasana can't hold a candle to the comfort of your generous heart. Brock and Clay, thank you both for helping me with my digital distractions and providing the best reason for me to unplug and be present. I'll always treasure every moment with you. Let breath bring you as much wonder and strength as it has given me. With each deep breath you take, a piece of me will always be with you. All my love.

Thank you to each and every reader of this book who begins to take 3DB and share the simple yet powerful energy of *Breathing Like a Boss*. We *can* make a global shift to a more mindful collective energy in business.

Namaste and much success!

ABOUT THE AUTHOR

SANDY ABRAMS is a longtime entrepreneur (founder of Moisture Jamzz), a small-business consultant, the author of *Your Idea, Inc.* (Adams, 2009), and a contributor to HuffPost and Thrive Global, writing about entrepreneurs, small business, and breath, yoga, and wellness. Abrams credits her entrepreneurial success to her nearly thirty years of yoga and breath practice that began in 1989. She completed yoga teacher training at the renowned Center for Yoga on Larchmont in Los Angeles in 1995. Abrams has consulted as a small-business thought leader, content curator, and social influencer with brands like Capital One, LegalZoom, Sage Software, and Marriott. With her "Breathe Like a Boss!" workshops, Abrams is on a mission to empower entrepreneurs, employees, leaders, teams, and executives with the (underutilized) power of breath for success and mindfulness in business.

Connect with Sandy:

Twitter & Instagram: *@sandyabrams*

Facebook: *https://www.facebook.com/SandyAbramsCEOm/*